How To

PERSONAL FINANCE

PAYING OFF YOUR MORTGAGE

How to choose and change
mortgage options to save money

Tony Cornell

How To Books

Cartoons by Mike Flanagan

British Library Cataloguing in Publication Data
A catalogue record for this book is available from the British Library.

© Copyright 1998 Tony Cornell.

First published in 1998 by How To Books Ltd, 3 Newtec Place,
Magdalen Road, Oxford OX4 1RE, United Kingdom.
Tel: (01865) 793806. Fax: (01865) 248780.
email: info@howtobooks.co.uk
www.howtobooks.co.uk

All rights reserved. No part of this work may be reproduced or stored in an information retrieval system (other than short extracts for the purposes of review) without the express permission of the Publishers given in writing.

Note: The material contained in this book is set out in good faith for general guidance and no liability can be accepted for loss or expense incurred as a result of relying in particular circumstances on statements made in the book. The law and regulations are complex and liable to change, and readers should check the current position with the relevant authorities before making personal arrangements.

Produced for How To Books by Deer Park Productions.
Edited by Julie Nelson.
Typeset by PDQ Typesetting, Stoke-on-Trent, Staffs.
Printed and bound by Cromwell Press, Trowbridge, Wiltshire.

Contents

List of illustrations		8
Preface		9
1	**Controlling your financial future**	**13**
	Grasping hold of the present	13
	Reality check	15
	Awareness of the mortgage	16
	Grasping hold of your future	16
	Case studies	17
	Questions and answers	18
	Personal mortgage audit	19
2	**Understanding the mortgage**	**20**
	Utilising knowledge to your advantage	20
	Defining a mortgage	21
	Understanding a mortgage	21
	Understanding interest rates	23
	Differentiating between interest calculation and interest charging	25
	Knowing the different interest rates available	30
	Avoiding redemption penalties	32
	Benefiting from mortgage tax relief (MIRAS)	35
	Mortgage indemnity guarantee premiums	37
	Considering mortgage protection insurance	39
	Case studies	40
	Questions and answers	42
	Personal mortgage audit	43
3	**Using the traditional banking system**	**44**
	Analysing traditional mortgage loans	44
	Understanding the traditional banking system	46
	Calculating the cost of the traditional banking system	47
	Case studies	49
	Questions and answers	50
	Personal mortgage audit	51

4	**Uncovering traditional mortgage loans**	52
	The standard capital repayment mortgage	52
	The interest-only mortgage	54
	Utilising an endowment policy	55
	Utilising a personal equity plan	57
	The individual savings account (ISA)	58
	Utilising a pension	58
	Examining mortgage incentives	59
	Avoiding ties and compulsories	60
	Case studies	61
	Questions and answers	61
	Personal mortgage audit	62
5	**Utilising traditional mortgage reduction methods**	63
	Increasing your deposit	63
	Reducing the term of a mortgage	65
	Making your payments fortnightly	65
	Making your payments weekly	66
	Increasing your repayment	67
	Making lump sum payments	68
	Consolidating your debts	69
	Splitting a mortgage	70
	Utilising savings plans and investments	71
	Case studies	73
	Questions and answers	73
	Personal mortgage audit	74
6	**Profiting from a flexible mortgage**	75
	Benefiting from a flexible mortgage	76
	Capitalising on a current account mortgage	80
	Utilising a credit card to reduce interest costs	83
	Case studies	84
	Questions and answers	85
	Personal mortgage audit	86
7	**Choosing the right lender**	87
	Uncovering the Mortgage Code	87
	Analysing the various mortgage lenders	90
	Considering other mortgage providers	93
	Utilising mortgage advisers	94
	Case studies	96
	Questions and answers	97
	Personal mortgage audit	97

	Contents	7

8	**Establishing a mortgage**	98
	Purchasing your first home	98
	Adding up the costs of buying and selling a property	99
	Refinancing your present mortgage	102
	Dealing with negative equity	106
	Choosing the mortgage and lender you want to use	107
	Calculating how much you can borrow	108
	Submitting a mortgage application	112
	Handling a rejected application	114
	Case studies	116
	Questions and answers	119
	Personal mortgage audit	119
9	**Managing your mortgage**	120
	Checking your mortgage statement	120
	Making a complaint	121
	Locating help for financial difficulties	122
	Case studies	123
	Questions and answers	124
	Personal mortgage audit	125
Glossary		126
Useful addresses		130
Further reading		133
Index		134

List of Illustrations

1	An example of the true cost of interest	45
2	The traditional banking system flowchart	47
3	The cost of interest and tax on your income	48
4	Traditional capital repayment mortgage graph	53
5	Comparison between monthly and fortnightly repayments	66
6	The effect of increasing the monthly repayment	67
7	Creating a surplus of funds	77
8	The new way of banking flowchart	81
9	Utilising a current account mortgage	82
10	Calculating the costs of buying and selling a property	103
11	Calculating the costs of refinancing	105
12	Calculating your gross income	109
13	Income multiplier	109
14	An expenses checklist	111
15	Obtaining your credit reference, letter template	117

Preface

For most of us, buying a home will be one of the largest purchases we will make in our lifetime, yet many people don't even give the mortgage a second thought. This ignorance can cost someone thousands to tens of thousands of pounds during a working life – but this does not have to be the case. Whether you have a mortgage, or are presently looking for one, this informative book will show you how you can utilise a mortgage to your advantage, rather than letting it work against you. In the process you will take years off the period of loan and save thousands of your hard-earned pounds.

Merely looking for a mortgage in the current highly competitive market can be quite a daunting task. There are presently over 200 mortgage providers and over 2,000 different mortgage products on offer. This rapidly increasing plethora of lenders and mortgage products has resulted in confusion for many. Written in a jargon-free style, this book will remove the confusion. It explains in plain English everything from finding the right lender, selecting and applying for the right mortgage, avoiding fees and charges, understanding interest rates, to utilising the new 'Aussie rules' interest methods and understanding how various interest calculation and charging methods greatly affect the amount you repay. Most importantly, this book will teach you how to pay a mortgage off in half the time or less, without dramatically changing your lifestyle.

I would like to thank Derek Watson for all his help and my lovely fiancée Natalie for her support and encouragement whilst writing this book.

Tony Cornell

This book will help you to:

- Pay off your mortgage in half the time or less.

- Dramatically reduce the amount of interest and fees you pay.

- Assert yourself as an educated and informed buyer.

- Improve your standard of lifestyle.

- Take control of your financial future.

- Learn more about various mortgage loans.

- Apply for and establish the right mortgage the first time.

- Utilise credit cards correctly to help you increase your savings.

- Avoid hidden clauses and unnecessary charges.

- Reduce the amount of tax you pay on savings accounts.

- Retire in a house you own with no money worries.

- Refinance your present mortgage.

- Learn how interest is calculated and charged on a mortgage.

1
Controlling Your Financial Future

> Success is a journey, not a destination...
> *Ben Sweetland*

In the United Kingdom millions of home buyers are paying at least twice the amount of interest and charges that they should be paying. This is due mainly to a lack of knowledge about mortgages. This lack of knowledge very often results in poor judgement on the part of the borrower and can cost them thousands of pounds over the term of a mortgage. This unnecessary loss of life earnings is totally irrecoverable.

Many books have been written about finances, budgeting, goal-setting and loans. Yet very few books have concentrated purely on mortgages, how they work, and how people can use them and the financial system to their advantage. This book will teach you how to turn the tables on the financial institutions, providing you with the necessary knowledge to reduce the amount of interest and charges you will repay. However, knowledge without action is worthless. Those of you who make the effort could save a fortune.

GRASPING HOLD OF THE PRESENT

Unfortunately for today's mortgage holders, the future may not offer the same safety nets that the past has provided. Various reasons account for the changed situation:

- The ageing of Britain's population and the eventual phasing out of the government-backed pension. Each individual will come to be responsible for their own future retirement income over and above their national insurance contributions.

- More and more people these days are working on a contract, casual and/or part-time basis, rather than the traditional full-time basis. The job-for-life culture is fast disappearing and this only adds to the insecurity of many.

- The European Union is still in its infancy and as yet is an unknown quantity. The effects of this partnership are yet to be seen.

- As many of us have experienced over the past ten years, the world's economy seems to be more and more erratic. As a result the future is uncertain and highly unpredictable. Many people do not know where to put their money, without the risk of losing it.

- Unlike the boom years of the past, experts are predicting lower capital growth on properties over the coming years due to a lower inflationary global economy.

There are literally dozens of reasons why the future in many cases has become an unknown quantity, and the above list covers only a handful of them. Life would be so simple if everyone owned a crystal ball to help them plan for their future. If this was possible, a good majority of people would stand a fairly good chance of succeeding financially in life. Unfortunately this is not possible, so you must realise the importance of planning for your future. This can only be achieved by grasping hold of your present situation and starting your financial planning **now** rather than later. By looking after the present, the future will take care of itself.

You may have already seen similar figures to those given below. They are a fairly accurate measurement of what people can expect in the future, if the past is anything to go by. If you do find yourself in the higher part of the following figures, then life is going to be terribly difficult for you in later years.

For 100 people presently aged 19, what will things be like at age 65? The forecast would look something like this:

38 will be dead

62 will be alive

Of those 62 people who will be alive at age 65:

38 will be broke

16 will still be working

7 will be retired on a liveable income

1 will be wealthy

These figures certainly paint a gloomy picture for a lot of people. However, it does not have to be this way. Let's look at why only a small percentage of people succeed financially. The 8 per cent of the population that do succeed and reach financial independence by age 65 all have certain qualities in common. If we were to isolate those qualities most prevalent within this select group, we would find that they:

- possessed *willingness to learn* and eagerly sought out knowledge that would help them achieve their life goals
- had a *plan* of some sort about where they were going
- set *goals* – and the majority wrote them down
- had *a good mental attitude* about what they were doing in their life and where they were headed
- lived within their means.

REALITY CHECK

1. If you do not *plan* for your retirement you could end up – like over 90 per cent of the population – either dead, dead broke, or still working. Chances are you may wake up one day and say, 'Where did the last 30 years go? I haven't achieved half the things I wanted to in my life.' By then it will be too late.

2. If you do not *set goals and write them down*, you will cruise through your life zig-zagging without any clear direction. This zigzag effect will cost you a lot of your precious present, a moment in time that is totally irrecoverable. Wouldn't you prefer to spend your precious present doing what you truly desire and looking back at every moment of time with fond memories?

3. Without *knowledge*, a *willingness to learn* and a *positive mental attitude* to change your lot in life, you will continue to do the same things that you have done in the past. By increasing and utilising your knowledge of a mortgage and the financial system, you will greatly increase your chances of achieving your dreams and life plan.

The above reality check is fairly hard hitting, but these are the cold, hard facts of life. You must realise how important it is to make a concerted effort to change what you are doing. If you do not, you will find yourself among the 90+ per cent and nothing you could ever do, other than receive a windfall, will get you out of it!

AWARENESS OF THE MORTGAGE

For many people living in the United Kingdom, buying a home will be one of the single largest purchases they will make in their lifetime. Many people, however, don't even give it a second thought and treat it as if they are buying a car or a stereo on finance. Properties are, of course, very costly and a mortgage can take a long time to repay. Bearing this in mind it is amazing how many people don't understand how a mortgage works, or how the interest calculation and charging method will dramatically affect the amount of interest they will pay. A mortgage can have a large impact on a person's financial future, if they do not understand it and use it properly.

A low APR and a welcome smile from your local high street bank does not necessarily mean the deal you are getting is a good one. A good majority of people are only concerned with how low the APR is. The disturbing thing is that many people don't even know what it stands for, or what it is exactly. APR is an abbreviation of Annual Percentage Rate and we cover this in more detail in the next chapter. There are over two thousand different mortgage products on the market today and this number is constantly rising. This is no doubt one of the main reasons why many people are confused and don't bother to educate themselves on this subject. If you do not understand how interest calculation and charging methods dramatically affect the amount you will pay, it will cost you a large percentage of your hard-earned income throughout the course of your life. The longer you leave it or ignore it, the more money you will lose.

GRASPING HOLD OF YOUR FUTURE

As discussed earlier in the chapter, times are changing and there is a lot more uncertainty in the world today. People in the past have relied heavily on a steady increase in their property value. This has resulted in many people becoming complacent about paying off their mortgage. Who was it that coined the phrase 'safe as houses'?

It would seem this person wasn't referring to the past ten years, as many people are well aware of the term **negative equity**. Gone are the days where you could rely on a steady increase in property values to help build equity in your home.

We are presently living through a low inflationary period and the experts are predicting that it will stay that way for some time yet. Within the present economic environment we unfortunately cannot rely on capital gains to build equity in the property. Rather, we must pay the mortgage off as quickly as possible to build the equity. A capital gain would then be seen as an added bonus. The following chapters will provide you with the necessary knowledge to:

- find the right lender and the right mortgage
- dramatically reduce fees and charges
- understand the importance of interest calculation and charging methods
- pay a mortgage off as quickly as possible.

By having this knowledge you can utilise the financial institutions to your advantage, rather than disadvantage. This knowledge provides the vehicle which can take you to where you want to be, in control of your financial future.

CASE STUDIES

Natalie wants to purchase an investment property

Natalie is 32 and is a self-employed business consultant. She is presently paying off her home. Being an ambitious and hard-working person, Natalie would like to put her earnings to better use and increase her personal wealth by investing in property. She currently has a PEP mortgage which she initially chose for the tax benefits. She wasn't overly concerned that it was linked to the stock market, as she tends to be a risk-taker. She is now concerned that the PEP will not perform well enough to provide sufficient returns to pay off the mortgage within the time frame she now wants. Paying off her present mortgage will allow her to purchase an investment property. She has decided to start shopping for a mortgage that will allow her to pay as often as she likes with the ability to reduce dramatically the term of the mortgage, without having to rely on an investment or savings plan.

John makes a positive move towards retirement

John is 48 and married with two children. He is a policeman and has been in the force for over 27 years. He currently has an endowment mortgage which he has been paying for the past 6 years. Recently his financial adviser rang him and told him that the endowment policy was not performing well enough to provide sufficient returns to repay the mortgage. This now means John will have to either increase his premiums or take out another policy to cover any possible shortfall. The prospects of still having a mortgage to pay at retirement is a major concern to John. Being rather conservative by nature, John has decided to refinance his endowment mortgage to a lower risk mortgage which has the facility for rapid capital reduction.

Ross seeks stability with flexibility

Ross is 25 and has recently married Cinzia. Ross and Cinzia are now looking for their first home and are confused about the different interest rates and various mortgage types on offer. Finding the right mortgage is important to them as Cinzia will be giving up work in the near future to give birth to their first child. With the prospects of a reduced income and added expenses, they will be on a tight budget for some time. Therefore, it is important for them to find a mortgage that will ensure their financial stability and also provide reasonable flexibility during this difficult period and beyond.

QUESTIONS AND ANSWERS

I can't earn enough money, how can I afford to plan for the future?

If you don't earn enough money to enable you to plan for the future, then strict budgeting and financial planning is going to be very important for you. By establishing goals and having a burning desire to achieve them, you will provide yourself with the necessary motivation to increase your knowledge to get a promotion or a better paying job.

Is it worthwhile to start planning for my future and set goals if I only have a few years until I retire?

A great deal can be achieved in only a few years with a little concentration and commitment. You can greatly improve your retirement years by setting goals to provide that little bit extra for when you do retire. Life doesn't end at retirement and for many people it will be a new chapter in their life. Retirement should be seen by many as the longest holiday in their life and a holiday without sufficient spending money is no holiday.

PERSONAL MORTGAGE AUDIT

- What type of mortgage do you presently have, or which one are you considering? Does this mortgage provide you with enough flexibility and allow for overpayments and increased frequency of payments?

- What is your present situation and where do you see yourself in 5, 10 and 15 years time?

- Do you currently set goals? If not, what would you like to achieve and when do you want to achieve it?

- What financial position would you like to be in at retirement age? Is your mortgage guaranteed to be repaid before retirement?

2
Understanding the Mortgage

It is costly wisdom that is bought by experience...
Learning teacheth more in one year than experience in twenty.
Roger Ascham: The Schoolmaster

UTILISING KNOWLEDGE TO YOUR ADVANTAGE

The education system has provided many of us with enough knowledge to join the workforce and earn an income. Unfortunately, throughout this whole process very few people were educated in the principles of finance, money management, budgeting and how the banking system works. It's a case of learning Financial Ju Jitsu, self-defence against financial institutions. This book will teach you and it won't hurt a bit! So consider this, you are about to embark on the finance lesson you never received at school. This lesson will save you big money and you will learn how to keep even more of it.

This chapter is the most important chapter in this book. Without a clear understanding of it, you will find it hard to grasp the principles outlined in the following chapters. If you do skip a part because you cannot understand it, ask your partner, a relative or even your boss to explain it to you. This may seem a little extreme, but the part you don't understand or the section you skip could effectively cost you thousands of pounds in savings. So treat this book as your course manual and study its contents in detail. It will certainly provide you with the most valuable knowledge, which could change your life for the better, for ever. This chapter will cover the **basic elements of a mortgage** which will enable you to:

- understand a mortgage and select the right repayment method
- choose the right interest rate with the best calculation and charging method
- avoid expensive penalties, fees and charges

- benefit from mortgage subsidies and make informed decisions on insurance products relevant to a mortgage.

DEFINING A MORTGAGE

The word 'mortgage' comes from a combination of two old French words, *mort* meaning death and *gage* meaning pledge. Originally a mortgage was a pledge or promise to repay a borrowed amount of money. Once this amount of money was repaid, the contractual agreement subsequently terminated and died.

Defining the terms 'mortgagor' and 'mortgagee'

A **mortgagor** is the financial institution lending the money. The **mortgagee** is the entity borrowing the money, whether a natural person, a company or whatever. The easiest way to remember the difference between the two would be to compare it with the employer and employee relationship. To keep things simple, throughout this book the mortgagor will be referred to as the **lender** and the mortgagee will be referred to as the **borrower**.

UNDERSTANDING A MORTGAGE

To understand fully how a mortgage works and how to use it to your advantage, you must first grasp the concept that there are many parts that make up a mortgage. Each part will affect the amount of interest you will repay. By arming yourself with this knowledge you can dramatically reduce the interest charges. A mortgage is comprised of the following:

1. the amount borrowed
2. the scheduled repayment term
3. the repayment method
4. the interest rate.

The amount borrowed

The amount borrowed is commonly referred to as the **capital** or **principal**. The more money you borrow, the more interest you will pay for the use of these funds. The interest calculated on an amount of £10,000.00 will obviously be less than on an amount of £20,000.00.

The scheduled repayment term
Traditionally a mortgage has been set over a 20- to 25-year time period. The period of time the borrowed money is spread over is referred to as the **amortization period**. The longer the repayment term, the smaller the monthly repayment. The shorter the repayment term, the higher the monthly repayment. Obviously the longer the repayment term the more interest you will pay. The shorter the repayment term the less interest you will repay. For example, if you borrowed an amount of £10,000.00 over a term of 10 years, assuming an interest rate of 8.00 per cent, your repayments would be £121.33 per month. The interest you will pay over this term would be £4,559.60. By extending this term to 20 years, the monthly repayment will decrease to £83.64 per month and the total interest payable would increase to £10,073.60 (see Chapter 5, Reducing the term of a mortgage).

The repayment method
Before you choose a mortgage you must determine which repayment method best suits your needs. Primarily there are only two repayment methods for a mortgage:

1. capital and interest repayment
2. interest-only repayment.

Capital and interest repayment
A portion of the borrower's repayment goes towards interest charges and a portion is paid off the capital. As each repayment is made the capital is subsequently reduced and less interest is charged, until the original amount borrowed is paid in full (see Chapter 4, The standard capital repayment mortgage).

Interest-only repayment
As the name suggests, only interest payments are required. None of the borrower's repayments are used to reduce the capital. Consequently the original amount financed will never reduce and the capital will always remain static. Endowment policies, savings plans and a pension can be used to repay the amount borrowed (as discussed in Chapter 4).

Variations
Although in principal there are only these two mortgage repayment methods, there can be many variations. Lenders today are breaking

old restraints and are becoming more flexible. Some lenders now offer combined features and benefits of the two repayment methods, such as allowing the borrower to make *minimum* interest payments only, but also giving the borrower the choice of paying the capital off as well. There are no hard and fast rules in this highly competitive market.

UNDERSTANDING INTEREST RATES

What is an 'interest rate'?
An interest rate is the cost for the use of borrowed money expressed as a percentage. The interest rate is charged on the amount you borrow (the **capital** or **principal** of the loan). The interest rate is not to be confused with an APR. The APR incorporates all fees and charges associated with the loan.

What is an APR?
APR is an abbreviation for **Annual Percentage Rate** and was legally implemented by the government in 1987. It is the official formula used by financial institutions to provide consumers with the true annual cost of a loan, expressed as a percentage. Basically the APR incorporates all the associated costs of the loan, such as the interest payable, redemption penalties, valuation fees, mortgage indemnity guarantee, any compulsory insurances and so on. A very basic example of this would be as follows:

Annualised charges:
Interest rate	8.00 %
Fees	.50 %
Other charges	.25 %
Annual Percentage Rate	8.75 %

This provides the borrower with an accurate system 'benchmark' for comparing between various lenders the total cost of a loan over an annual period.

Prior to the APR being implemented, lenders would offer low interest rates. However, the lenders were not clearly disclosing the additional fees and charges applicable to the loan. Consequently, the borrower would think they were getting a bargain, when in fact they were not. The APR reduces the need for the borrower to understand colourful and at times deceptive jargon used by lenders.

An example of this is the use of the term 'economic adjustment', one of many terms used by lenders as a replacement for the word 'fee' or 'charge'.

APR and the mortgage
It is worth noting that when lenders calculate an APR they may use the initial introductory discounted or fixed rate. Discounted or fixed interest rates usually only apply for a short time period and the prevailing interest rate after the discounted or fixed period may be higher. Consequently this does not provide the borrower with a truly accurate measurement of the total cost of the mortgage over the full term. The easiest way to determine the total cost of a mortgage would be to add up the total repayments over the full term and take into consideration the discounted or fixed rate period. When comparing a mortgage the APR may not in all cases be the best benchmark.

DIFFERENTIATING BETWEEN INTEREST CALCULATION AND INTEREST CHARGING

Before a lender can charge interest on the amount you have borrowed, they must first calculate how much interest to charge to the mortgage balance. The frequency with which interest is calculated and then charged will vary depending on the lender. For example, the interest may be calculated daily and then charged to the mortgage balance monthly, or the interest may be calculated yearly and then charged to the mortgage yearly.

It is not necessary to know the complex financial equations they use. It is, however, vitally important that you understand the difference between calculating interest and charging interest. After reading this book you will find that you will be more knowledgeable about how interest works, probably more than the lender's staff themselves. Don't believe everything you hear, only believe what you see in black and white. Always ask the lender for information in writing:

- a mortgage illustration
- a brochure
- an official letter from the lender, *or*
- the loan agreement itself.

Although the interest calculation and charging method forms one formula, they have been divided into two, to simplify things. The next two sections will explain the most common **interest calculation** and **interest charging** methods used by lenders today. (Lenders do not actively promote the interest calculation and charging method used.)

Calculating interest on a mortgage

A large number of mortgage lenders, in particular building societies, have calculated interest on a mortgage for the whole year. Basically the interest is calculated on the balance you owe at the start of the yearly period. This is regardless of whether the balance you owe during the year reduces or not.

You may have heard about the '**Aussie Rules**' interest calculation and charging methods on television, or read various articles in magazines and newspapers. It certainly has placed the spotlight on those lenders who calculate and charge the interest yearly. In Australia, the majority of lenders calculate the interest daily on a reducing balance and then charge the interest to the mortgage monthly in arrears. Thankfully more and more lenders in the United Kingdom are starting to calculate and charge their interest this way. Daily interest calculation with monthly charging methods are much fairer for the borrower than yearly calculation and charging methods. With the Aussie Rules method, more frequent repayments such as fortnightly or by making lump sum payments will reduce the balance accordingly (see Figure 5 which shows a typical comparison between monthly and fortnightly repayments). The interest is then calculated on the reduced balance daily and this calculated interest is then charged to the mortgage the following month.

Calculating interest daily
Interest calculated daily on a reducing balance is the best calculation method for any mortgage which allows capital reduction. As mentioned earlier, the interest calculation and charging methods normally only apply to a capital repayment mortgage. Many interest-only mortgages do not allow capital reduction and the balance will usually remain static.

With the daily interest calculation method, when you make a payment to the mortgage the balance will subsequently reduce. The interest is then calculated on this reduced balance the following day. As a result the interest calculated will be less than the previous day. To calculate daily interest you must first multiply the outstanding loan balance by the interest rate (not the APR), and then divide this figure by 365 being the number of days in a year. The daily interest calculation formula is:

$$\frac{\text{(outstanding loan balance} \times \text{interest rate)}}{365 \text{ days}}$$

Using the example above, based on an outstanding loan balance of £60,000.00 with an interest rate of 8.50 per cent per annum, the calculation would look like this:

$$\frac{(£60,000.00 \times 8.50\%)}{365 \text{ days}} = £13.97 \text{ daily interest}$$

Taking this a stage further, let's see what effect making a payment of £500.00 will have on the amount of interest calculated on the following day:

Day 1
Mortgage balance day 1   £60,000.00
Interest calculated day 1   £13.97
Repayment day 1   £500.00

Day 2
Mortgage balance day 2   £59,500.00
Interest calculated day 2   £13.86

As you can see from the above example, by making a payment of £500.00 the outstanding balance has reduced to £59,500.00. This has resulted in an interest saving of 11 pence on the following day. This 11 pence saving will continue every day, until the interest **calculated for the month** is then **charged** to the mortgage balance. Obviously the longer the lender takes to charge the interest to the mortgage the better.

Should you make additional repayments prior to the interest being charged, the interest calculated will then be reduced further (discussed in more detail in Chapter 5). You can save enormous amounts of interest using this calculation method, as opposed to 'in the lender's favour' monthly and yearly interest calculation methods.

This is true so long as:

- the particular lender allows you to pay as often as you like, with no limitations on payment frequency
- the lender allows lump sum payments to be made
- there are no partial redemption penalties for overpayments on the mortgage.

There are lenders that calculate the interest daily, but they may not apply the payments to the mortgage immediately. If the payments are not credited to the outstanding balance immediately, most of the benefit of daily interest calculation method will be lost.

Calculating interest monthly
Monthly interest calculation is not quite as bad as the 'yearly' calculation method. However, it still does not provide the same level

of savings as the daily reducible calculation method. When a repayment is made and the outstanding balance is reduced, the interest is not calculated on the reduced balance until the end of the month. Therefore, increasing the repayment frequency or increasing the amount paid during the month will not benefit the borrower until the end of the month. The monthly interest calculation formula is virtually the same as the daily method, the only difference being that, rather than dividing by 365 days, you would divide by twelve (the number of months in a calendar year).

Calculating interest yearly
Many lenders calculate interest on a mortgage for the whole year, on the balance you owe at the start of the period, regardless of whether or not the mortgage balance reduces during this period. This in effect is pre-calculated interest charges and should be avoided at all costs. This interest calculation method benefits everyone except the borrower. The only advice to you, should your mortgage have interest calculated this way, would be to move the mortgage to another lender that provides the daily reducible interest calculation method.

Charging interest to a mortgage
Once the interest has been calculated on a mortgage, the lender will then charge this interest to the loan balance. The frequency with which interest is charged will vary considerably between lenders. The interest charging frequency will also affect the amount of interest you will repay. There are primarily two types of interest charging methods used today:

1. interest charged in advance
2. interest charged in arrears.

Charging interest in advance
Many building societies and some banks, as discussed earlier, calculate and charge the interest on a mortgage for the whole year. This in effect is pre-calculated interest and regardless of whether the lender charges the interest to the mortgage balance monthly, quarterly or yearly in advance, it is totally unacceptable.

Charging interest in arrears
This is the only satisfactory interest charging method. It is completely the reverse of interest charged in advance. Some

Understanding the Mortgage

lenders charge the interest to the mortgage monthly in arrears and some charge quarterly in arrears. Quarterly in this context refers to a quarter of one year, i.e. every three months. The longer the lender takes to charge the interest to the mortgage balance the better. Monthly and quarterly in arrears charging methods are fast becoming the industry standard. The larger banks and building societies will be slower to conform, but market pressures and increasing competition from other direct competitors will eventually force them to follow suit.

Examining interest calculation and charging

Let's take a closer look at the way interest is **calculated** and then **charged** to the mortgage balance. The following example is based on a standard capital repayment mortgage. The interest rate is 8.50 per cent per annum which is calculated monthly and charged monthly in arrears, to keep things simple. The amount borrowed is £80,000.00 over a 25-year term. The monthly repayments will be £644.18 gross (not including MIRAS subsidy, see page 35).

Year 1
Balance 'Month 1'		£80,000.00
Monthly repayment	£644.18	
Interest charge	£566.67	
Capital reduction	£77.51	
Balance owing end of 'Month 1'		£79,922.49
Monthly repayment 'Month 2'	£644.18	
Interest charge	£566.11	
Capital reduction	£78.07	
Balance owing end of 'Month 2'		£79,844.42

After 5 years
Balance owing 'Month 1', Year5		£74,347.27
Monthly repayment	£644.18	
Interest charge	£526.63	
Capital reduction	£117.55	
Balance owing end of 'Month 1'		£74,229.72

As you can see from the example, your loan repayments are paid in each month thus reducing the balance outstanding. Interest is then **calculated** monthly on this reduced balance. Once a month the interest is then **charged** to the mortgage balance. The monetary difference between the monthly repayment and the interest charged, is known as the **capital reduction**. This capital reduction over time reduces the capital owing as each payment is made. Subsequently as the capital reduces, the interest charges will decrease. **This is the most critical aspect to understand**. That is the way interest is calculated on a reducing balance. Without a clear understanding of this, you will find it hard to grasp the concepts outlined in this book.

KNOWING THE DIFFERENT INTEREST RATES AVAILABLE

Understanding variable rates
The interest rate is not fixed and will fluctuate with the market. When interest rates move, depending on market conditions, the variable rate can rise and can also fall. When interest rates rise, so will your monthly mortgage repayment. Should they fall, so will your monthly mortgage repayment.

Utilising the annualised repayment scheme
Many lenders offer annualised repayment schemes or annually adjusted mortgages. Under this scheme the monthly repayments are adjusted annually, rather than when the interest rates change. This allows the borrower to budget knowing their repayments are set and will not increase for a twelve-month period. If the interest rates do change, the amount of interest charged on the mortgage will increase or decrease, yet your monthly repayments will not change. At the end of the twelve-month period, your monthly repayments will then be adjusted for the next twelve months. These new repayments will take into consideration any overpayments or underpayments made in the prior year, as a result of any rise or fall in the interest rate. The only disadvantage would be that, when the annual adjustment for the following year has been completed, the new annualised monthly repayments may rise dramatically, because of rises in interest rates during the prior year.

> **Lenders who offer this type of scheme generally calculate and charge interest in advance.**

Understanding fixed rates
In this type of scheme, the interest rate is fixed for a set period. Generally the fixed rate period will be one to five years. After the

fixed term expires the interest rate will usually revert to the prevailing standard variable rate at that time. Fixed interest rates protect the borrower when interest rates rise. However, should interest rates fall the borrower could end up being locked into a higher rate. For example, you fixed the interest rate at 8 per cent. If interest rates rose above 8 per cent, the fixed interest rate would not rise and you would be protected. If, on the other hand, interest rates fell below 8 per cent, you would be locked into a higher rate and would not enjoy the lower rates. Other things to be mindful of are:

- Fixed rates generally have very **high redemption penalties** should the borrower wish to pay off the mortgage in full during the fixed rate period. These penalties may apply for several years even after the fixed rate period has ended.
- It is important to ensure the fixed rate mortgage is **portable**. That is, should you wish to move house during the fixed rate period, you can transfer the mortgage to the new address and not incur any redemption penalties.

Understanding capped and collared rates

Some mortgage lenders offer **capped rates**. Basically they guarantee that the interest rate will not rise above a certain rate for a fixed period of time. Should rates fall, however, the capped interest rate will also fall. For example, if the variable rate at the time was 8 per cent, the lender may cap it at 10 per cent. This protects the borrower should interest rates rise above 10 per cent and allows the borrower to enjoy lower rates should they fall.

A lender may accompany the capped rate with a **collar**. A collar basically prevents the interest rate falling below a set rate. Adding to the example above, the lender may collar it at 6 per cent. So effectively you would be locked between a collared rate of 6 per cent and a capped rate of 10 per cent. Capped rates *without* the collar have certain benefits over traditional fixed rates. They protect the borrower should interest rates rise and allow the borrower to enjoy the lower rates should interest rates fall.

Things to look out for:

- administration fees can be quite high
- redemption penalties may apply to partial and full discharge of the mortgage.

Understanding discounted rates

In this type of scheme, the lender will discount their standard variable rate by a certain percentage. For example, if the standard variable rate was 8 per cent, the lender may offer a 2 per cent discount, effectively making the discounted rate 6 per cent. Generally the discount will be for a short period of time and this varies from a few months to three years depending upon the lender. After the discount period ends, the interest rate will usually revert back to the standard variable rate prevailing at the time. However, this is not always the case and the interest rate after the discount period may be higher, so check first.

This form of interest rate deal is generally marketed to first home buyers offering them initially lower monthly repayments. Discounted rates are also commonly referred to within the mortgage market as **honeymoon rates**. This is because once the honeymoon, i.e. being the lower rate period, is over, the borrower is locked into the higher rate, the marriage. Lenders also offer these type of interest rate deals to people with substantial equity in their property as an enticement to change lenders. When the market is down, lenders will offer discounted rates to entice people to take their mortgage. Some things to be mindful of when looking at discounted rates are:

- Redemption penalties may apply to full and partial discharge of the mortgage.

- You should ensure the mortgage is portable. That is, should you wish to move house during the fixed rate period, you can transfer the mortgage to the new address and not incur any redemption penalties.

- The lender may require the borrower to repay the discount in full should the borrower move their mortgage to another lender during the discounted period.

AVOIDING REDEMPTION PENALTIES

These penalties are imposed by lenders to discourage borrowers from paying off the mortgage before the set term of the loan agreement. Many lenders for some time have offered mortgage deals and incentives such as cash back, discounted rates, capped rates and fixed interest rates. When a lender offers a special deal or incentive, they cover themselves by imposing redemption penalties. It's an attempt to stop the customer paying off their mortgage after the offer ends and subsequently refinancing with another lender. It's the lender's way of ensuring they will get their 'two bobs' worth and of protecting their own interest.

These penalties can apply to partial ('part') redemption of the mortgage by making an overpayment and/or a lump sum payment, or to full redemption of the mortgage balance ('discharge'), also known as **early payout penalties**.

Calculating the costs of redemption

The redemption penalties that can be imposed will vary from lender to lender. The period of time they can be enforced will usually be up to five years from the loan commencement date. Some lenders set the enforcement period at as many as seven or more years, so watch out. Listed below are the most common redemption penalties being imposed at present. This will give you a fairly good idea of the variety of ways by which lenders calculate them.

- Monthly interest calculation method – the lender can charge anything from 3 to 6 months penalty interest. Some lenders may charge more.

- A lender may charge you a percentage of the balance owed on the mortgage at the time of payment. This penalty can be up to 6 per cent or even greater.

- The lender may charge a percentage of the actual amount being paid. This penalty can be anything from 2.5 to 6 per cent of the payment amount or even greater.

- The lender can reclaim the discounted interest rate difference given.

- The lender can claim any cash back given to the customer under an incentive scheme.

As you can see from the redemption penalty methods listed, lenders can very easily change your mind about paying off their mortgage. A mortgage of £60,000.00 with a 6 per cent of balance calculation equates to £3,600.00 in redemption charges. The worst case scenario could be if you are forced to sell your house as a result of losing your job, and then get whacked with a redemption penalty. Let's look at partial and full redemption penalties in more detail.

Partial redemption penalties

These redemption penalties apply to 'over-payments and/or lump sum payments' made over and above the standard monthly mortgage repayment. In effect you are only partially redeeming the mortgage balance by making a partial payment. Many lenders do not allow borrowers to make overpayments or lump sum payments at all. However, there are lenders that do allow overpayments and lump sum payments without imposing any penalties. These lenders, however, may impose restrictions on the borrower by setting minimum and maximum repayment amounts allowable. This in effect restricts the borrower from paying the mortgage off faster. As a result this reduces the borrower's potential savings and ensures the lender will make their profit target.

Full redemption penalties

Full redemption penalties are also known as **early payout penalties**. These penalties apply to the full discharge of the mortgage. Full redemption penalties are prevalent with fixed interest rates, capped rates, discounted rates, cash back and also on some standard variable mortgage loans.

Should you decide to pay off your mortgage early, you will have to weigh up the costs of early redemption against the overall savings achieved by refinancing to another mortgage. For example, if interest rates drop dramatically and you are locked into a high fixed interest rate, it may be worth while paying off the current fixed rate mortgage and moving to a lower rate mortgage. This should only be done if the overall savings even after the redemption penalties are greater.

Words of warning:

- The best mortgage redemption penalties are none at all!
- Before you sign any mortgage agreement make sure you are absolutely sure of any redemption penalties that may apply.

There are plenty of lenders in the United Kingdom that do not impose any penalties at all. So when you are shopping for a mortgage, choose carefully and leave redemption penalties off the list.

BENEFITING FROM MORTGAGE TAX RELIEF (MIRAS)

The government currently provides tax relief on mortgages known as MIRAS, which is an acronym for Mortgage Interest Relief At Source. MIRAS provides a 10 per cent subsidy on the interest charges for the first £30,000.00 borrowed. This subsidy is restricted to the main residential property only. The interest charged over and above £30,000.00 is not subsidised and is paid in full by the borrower.

Mortgage tax relief was reduced from 15 per cent to 10 per cent in April 1998. The level of tax relief provided by the government has slowly eroded over the years. Prior to 5 April 1994, interest relief was granted at the basic rate of tax, i.e. 25 per cent. It is more than likely that MIRAS will be phased out completely in the not too distant future, so there goes that deduction.

Gross and net payments

You may have noticed that when a lender quotes payments, they will either be net payments or gross payments. Net payments have already had the MIRAS subsidy deducted. Gross repayments have not had any MIRAS tax relief deducted from the payments.

Gross interest

This means that the MIRAS subsidy has not been deducted from the interest and the subsidy has to be claimed by the borrower. (See below, Claiming MIRAS.) Let's look a little closer at how MIRAS is calculated. Assume an interest-only mortgage of £50,000.00 with an interest rate of 8 per cent per annum.

Calculate the monthly interest by using the monthly interest calculation:

$$\frac{£50{,}000.00 \times 8\%}{12 \text{ months}} = £333.33 \text{ gross monthly interest}$$

Net interest

Net interest is interest less the MIRAS subsidy on the qualifying portion of the loan amount, i.e. £30,000.00. Based on the previous example for gross interest, we will again assume an interest-only mortgage with a balance of £50,000.00, with an interest rate of 8 per cent per annum.

Step 1. Calculate the gross monthly interest on the qualifying MIRAS portion, i.e. the first £30,000.00, using the monthly interest calculation:

$$\frac{£30,000.00 \times 8\%}{12 \text{ months}} = £200.00 \text{ monthly gross interest}$$

Step 2. Subtract the 10% MIRAS subsidy from the qualifying gross interest:

Gross monthly interest of £200.00 − MIRAS of 10% = £180.00 net interest

Step 3. Calculate the gross monthly interest on the non-subsidised portion, i.e. £20,000.00:

$$\frac{£20,000.00 \times 8\%}{12 \text{ months}} = £133.33 \text{ gross monthly interest portion}$$

Step 4. Add the subsidised interest portion of £180.00 to the non-subsidised gross interest portion, i.e. £133.33. This will give you the net monthly interest:

£180.00 + £133.33 = £313.33 total net monthly interest

As you can see from the example above, the total interest saving using MIRAS is £20.00 per month.

Eligibility for MIRAS
MIRAS is normally only granted on your main home ('principal place of residence'), so long as it is in the United Kingdom or the Republic of Ireland. Houseboats and caravans also qualify if they are used as the main home. MIRAS is not granted in every circumstance, so check with the lender to see if you qualify.

Claiming MIRAS
The lender will usually provide the borrower with a MIRAS 70 form for new mortgages and a MIRAS 76 form for remortgages.

Understanding the Mortgage

These forms are then completed by the borrower. If the conditions on either form are not satisfied, the lender will then provide the borrower with a MIRAS 3 form to be completed. These forms are then sent to the tax office. The majority of lenders in the United Kingdom participate in the MIRAS scheme and the subsidy is deducted by the lender before you pay interest. The lender then recovers the difference from the government. Should the lender not be part of the MIRAS scheme, the interest is paid in full by the borrower. The borrower can then claim the tax relief on their yearly tax return.

MORTGAGE INDEMNITY GUARANTEE PREMIUMS

Mortgage indemnity guarantee insurance ('MIG'), protects the lender should the borrower default on the loan agreement, leading to the subsequent repossession of the property. MIG guarantees to pay the lender the shortfall between what the property is sold for and the outstanding mortgage balance.

Lenders normally charge a borrower a MIG premium or fee if the LTV ratio (or in plain English 'loan to value' ratio) is high. The LTV ratio is the actual amount borrowed expressed as a percentage of the property purchase price or property valuation (whichever is the lower). For example, if you borrowed an amount of £37,500.00 secured on a property valued at £50,000.00, the LTV ratio would be 75 per cent.

The loan to value ratio calculation is:

$$\frac{\text{Amount borrowed}}{\text{Property value}} \times 100 = \text{\% Loan to value ratio}$$

Using the example above:

$$\frac{£37,500.00}{£50,000.00} \times 100 = 75\% \text{ LTV ratio}$$

Consequently the LTV ratio on an amount borrowed of £80,000.00, secured on a property worth £80,000.00, would be 100 per cent.

In the United Kingdom lenders will usually lend up to 75 per cent of the LTV ratio. Loans exceeding 75 per cent of the loan to value ratio will usually be subject to a MIG premium or fee. Some lenders, however, may charge MIG starting from 80 per cent LTV ratio, and some may not charge anything at all. It will all depend upon the lender and the level of risk they wish to take. Lenders use a variety of names for MIG and a few examples are:

- additional security fee
- scheme for maximum advances
- high lending fee
- high percentage loan fee.

Unlike mortgage protection insurance, you cannot shop around for MIG premiums and fees, and the fees charged vary considerably between lenders. It may pay you to compare various lenders and weigh up the overall package on offer.

Costing MIG premiums
Not all lenders calculate MIG premiums and fees the same way. The amount of MIG premium or fees the borrower will pay will usually depend on:

1. the amount borrowed, and
2. the LTV ratio.

The higher the LTV ratio and the higher the amount borrowed, the more MIG premium or fees, will be charged. By paying a larger deposit you can reduce the amount of MIG premium or fees you will pay (see Chapter 5, increasing your deposit). The MIG premium or fees can be added to the loan, but this increases the amount borrowed and interest is subsequently charged on this amount. A borrower may also pay the MIG premium or fees separately.

It is interesting to note that the MIG premiums are not based on the borrower's creditworthiness. They are in fact based on the lender's creditworthiness. So a borrower could pay a larger fee because of a lender's poor lending history. In past years MIG insurance providers have sustained high claims resulting in large losses due to falling house prices, increasing unemployment levels and so on. Consequently MIG insurance premiums have increased substantially and some lenders have chosen to self-insure.

Understanding subrogation
Should a lender exercise their power of sale and repossess your home, they can then make a claim against the MIG insurance policy. The MIG insurance provider can then make a claim against you for the amount paid to the lender for the claim. In effect, you have paid the MIG premium or fees to protect the lender, yet these premiums paid have provided you with no protection at all. This unusual legal process is known as **subrogation**.

CONSIDERING MORTGAGE PROTECTION INSURANCE

Unlike MIG insurance, mortgage protection insurance covers the borrower not the lender and the premiums are still paid by the borrower. There are many different mortgage protection insurance policies available. Some of the most popular policies are:

- life insurance
- involuntary unemployment insurance
- sickness and disability insurance
- critical illness insurance.

Mortgage protection insurance can be quite expensive, but the benefits can prove invaluable in helping prevent financial difficulties should the borrower suffer from a major illness, redundancy, or any other unforeseen event.

Key benefits of this insurance are that it:

- reduces the risk of the property being repossessed
- protects the borrower's credit rating
- provides security for the family
- prevents financial hardship.

Choosing your insurance provider
Unlike life insurance and building insurance, mortgage protection insurance is not compulsory when taking out a mortgage. A borrower is also not obliged to take any insurance offered by the lender such as life, building, contents, or any mortgage protection

insurance. The borrower can shop around and choose any insurance provider and policy they wish. The only exception to this is when a lender offers a package deal and the insurance product forms part of the terms and conditions of the package, known as **ties** or **compulsories**. (See Chapter 4, avoiding ties and compulsories.)

Eligibility
In some cases a medical may be required prior to a policy being issued by the insurance provider. Mortgage protection insurance in most cases will not cover any pre-existing illness or pre-existing injuries.

Beware of exclusions, terms and conditions
- Beware of small print and make sure you read the terms and conditions before accepting the policy.
- Many policies can have unacceptable claim exclusions and rather lengthy payment terms.
- Life insurance, sickness and disability and critical illness insurance will generally not cover any pre-existing illness or any pre-existing injuries.
- Involuntary unemployment insurance usually requires the policy-holder to be in continuous employment for a minimum of two years. Involuntary unemployed insurance is not always available for self-employed persons.

The best advice would be to shop around for the best deal and take your time. This little bit of extra time spent looking may save you a lot of frustration and perhaps thousands in premium savings over the term of a mortgage.

CASE STUDIES

Natalie takes a risk
After considering the various options open to her, Natalie has decided on a variable rate of interest. She is looking for a lender that will calculate the interest daily and charge the interest either monthly or quarterly in arrears. Being a risk-taker she is not overly concerned with the possibility of the variable interest rate rising. Her income is good but at times can be irregular, so she likes the idea of paying as often as she likes. Consequently finding a

mortgage that does not have partial redemption penalties is a must for her. Natalie's intention to pay off her current mortgage as quickly as possible will mean there must not be any early redemption penalties on the new mortgage. Natalie has a reasonable amount saved in her savings account. She will use these savings to reduce the capital borrowed on the new mortgage. Because she will only be borrowing 70 per cent of the property value, there will be no MIG insurance payable on the new mortgage. Other than the statutory life insurance, she does not feel it is necessary to take out any mortgage protection insurance. Natalie has many insurance policies already in place should an unforeseen event occur.

John is cautious in his decision
Having weighed up the various interest rates on offer, John feels that the safest option will be either a fixed rate or a capped rate, without the collar. He is aware that these types of interest rates may attract early redemption penalties. The interest must be calculated daily and charged either monthly or quarterly in arrears. John's main goal is to pay off the mortgage before he retires, so he requires a reasonably flexible mortgage that will allow overpayments, with little or no redemption penalties. John has decided to take out disability, sickness and involuntary unemployment mortgage protection insurance. Because of his age the insurance company may ask John to take a medical. This added protection will cover himself and his family in case of any unforeseen events, which may greatly affect the goals he has set. He will also shop around for the best deal on the mortgage protection insurance.

Ross seeks stability
Since Ross's wife is due to have a baby within the next few months, Ross wants stability through this period, without any unexpected surprises. In consideration of this he has chosen a capped rate without the collar. The interest must be calculated daily and charged either monthly or quarterly in arrears. Because the interest rate will be capped for a reasonable period of time, his repayments will not increase as a result of any rises in interest rates. This will offset the need for the annualised repayment scheme. Ross and Cinzia have only saved enough money to provide a 10 per cent deposit. The loan to value ratio will be 90 per cent and this could mean the mortgage will be subject to MIG premiums. In addition to the statutory life insurance, Ross has decided to take out disability, sickness and involuntary unemployment mortgage protection. This

added protection will cover his family against any unforeseen events. Ross will shop around for the best mortgage protection deal.

QUESTIONS AND ANSWERS

How can I tell if interest rates are going to rise or fall so I will know whether to take out a fixed, capped or variable rate?

It is very hard even for the experts to predict whether interest rates will rise or fall. Interest rates are influenced by so many factors such as the economy, inflation rate, unemployment figures and so on. You have to look at your own personal situation and determine firstly whether you could afford to pay higher repayments should interest rates rise. If interest rates are already high, then it may be worth while to take a variable rate with the hope that interest rates will fall. Taking a fixed rate when interest rates are high could prove to be very expensive if they fall dramatically. If you look at your present situation and take your future requirements into consideration, you should make a fairly good personal decision.

My capital repayment mortgage has partial and full redemption penalties with the interest calculated and charged yearly in advance. Is it worth while refinancing it?

It may pay to refinance this type of mortgage to one that has the interest calculated daily and charged either monthly or quarterly in arrears. Firstly though, you must determine what the full redemption penalties will be to pay off the existing mortgage. Secondly you must determine what the associated costs will be in taking out the new mortgage. Thirdly you have to determine how much you will save with the new mortgage. If the total savings with the new mortgage far outweigh the costs of refinancing, then you should be able to make an informed decision whether you should refinance or not.

Does the interest calculation and charging method affect all mortgage types?

No, interest-only mortgages require the borrower to pay the interest charges which are calculated on the balance or capital outstanding. Many people rely on savings plans or investments to pay off the mortgage, and as a result they may choose not to reduce the capital during the term. If the capital is not reduced during the term, the interest calculation and charging method will have little or no effect. However, with a capital repayment mortgage, the interest calculation is vitally important as you pay a portion of capital and a portion of interest with every repayment. As your capital reduces you will pay less interest.

PERSONAL MORTGAGE AUDIT

- What **repayment method** are you using at present, or considering using? Which one would best suit your needs: interest only or capital repayment?

- If you presently have a mortgage or are considering one, what interest **calculation** and **charging** method is being used?

- Which type of **interest rate** would suit your particular circumstances the best. Variable, fixed, capped or discounted?

- Are there any **redemption penalties** which apply to either the full or partial redemption of the mortgage? Will these affect your present and future needs?

- Is **MIRAS** deducted from the interest before you make your repayments? If not, are you eligible and are you claiming this subsidy on your yearly tax return?

- Do you have **mortgage protection insurance** cover, or are you considering taking out this cover? Does your present and future situation warrant having this cover? Have you shopped around for the best deal?

3
Using the Traditional Banking System

> You don't drown by falling in the water.
> You drown by staying there.
>
> *Unknown*

Over the years you may have seen financial institutions report quarterly and annual record profits on television and in the newspapers. Financial institutions like any company are in business to make a profit. If you continue to use the traditional banking system the way you have in the past, you will continue contributing to these massive profits. As a result you will lose hundreds or thousands of your hard-earned pounds throughout the course of your life. By your own commitment to make a change and educate yourself about the mortgage, you have made a decision to reduce the amount of interest and charges you will repay. In doing so you will increase your own personal wealth by dramatic proportions.

ANALYSING TRADITIONAL MORTGAGE LOANS

The traditional banking system has offered various mortgage products to mainstream society granted either for personal or investment purposes. Generally they have been a capital repayment mortgage or an interest-only mortgage. The standard scheduled repayment term has been 20 to 25 years.

Let's take a closer look

The example in Figure 1 is based on a standard capital repayment mortgage. The interest rate is 9.50 per cent per annum, calculated daily on a reducing balance and charged monthly in arrears. The loan amount is £120,000.00 over a 25-year term, with monthly repayments of £1,050.00 gross of MIRAS.

As you can see from the example, after the first 12 months your total repayments would amount to £12,600.00, of which only

Using the Traditional Banking System 45

Year	Total yearly payments £	Capital £	Interest £	Balance £
1	12,600.00	1,342.00	11,258.00	118,658.00
2	25,200.00	2,709.00	22,491.00	117,291.00
5	63,000.00	7,680.00	55,320.00	112,320.00
10	126,000.00	16,935.00	109,065.00	103,065.00
15	189,000.00	34,705.00	154,295.00	85,295.00
20	252,000.00	62,789.00	189,211.00	56,175.00
25	315,000.00	120,000.00	195,000.00	00.00

Fig. 1. An example of the true cost of interest.

£1,342.00 reduces your capital and a whopping £11,258.00 is gobbled up in interest charges.

Do you remember when you first submitted your mortgage application, waiting anxiously by the phone for the loan approval to come through? The manager of the particular lender you chose would then confirm the mortgage details and tell you what your monthly repayments were. You would say the repayments are fine and would proceed to get very excited about moving into your new home. If the lender at the time told you that over the first twelve months £11,258.00 would be paid in interest and only £1,342.00 would reduce the capital, would you think they were joking?

If we look a little closer at this illustration, after ten years you would have paid back £126,000.00, of which £109,065.00 is paid in interest and a mere £16,935.00 is paid off your capital! It would be too bad if the housing market suffered a major drop in the 9th or 10th year bringing the property into negative equity.

People wonder why it's so hard to pay off their mortgage!

Many people do not realise how much a mortgage will actually cost them in interest charges, until their first mortgage statement arrives. Rather than educate themselves to reduce the amount of interest they repay, the majority of people accept this as the way it is, and the statement is subsequently filed.

Should you have an interest-only mortgage linked to an investment or savings plan such as a PEP, pension or endowment policy, then hopefully your particular investment will provide sufficient returns to repay the mortgage capital in the future. The future, however, is an unknown quantity at the best of times. When you repay an interest-only mortgage the lenders are in their element, receiving interest-only payments for up to 15 to 25 years. In many cases the capital over the set term will not reduce and the interest will be calculated on the initial amount borrowed. In addition to this the lender may also receive commissions from the investment or savings plan they supplied to you. There is growing concern that lenders may recommend an interest-only mortgage to their customers, even though a capital repayment mortgage may be more suitable. The profits a lender earns from an interest-only mortgage and the commissions received from the savings plan or investment they supplied far outweigh the profits earned from a capital repayment mortgage.

UNDERSTANDING THE TRADITIONAL BANKING SYSTEM

Financial institutions earn a great deal of their profits from the difference between what they *pay* for the money they borrow from customers and what they *charge* customers for the use of these funds. For example, if you invested £5,000.00 in a savings account, the financial institution may pay you 4 per cent interest on these funds. Effectively you have earned 4 per cent and this has cost the financial institution 4 per cent. The financial institution may then lend these funds out at 9 per cent, so the gross profit difference between what these funds cost them and what they earned would be 5 per cent.

Amount charged to a borrower for the use of these funds	9%
Cost of funds (what they paid you for the use of the funds)	4%
Gross profit difference, 'the fat'	5%

This profit difference is commonly referred to as **the fat**. Of course, financial institutions also earn their profits from a variety of other sources such as insurances, investments, travel and so on. The traditional banking system was designed to make money for the financial institution, not the customer. Many people today have their employer pay their wages directly into a current account via an electronic funds transfer. Once the wage is credited to the account people usually pay their mortgage repayment first. The amount left over is then used to pay the monthly bills. The fortunate and/or disciplined people may also transfer a bit into a savings account each month. This movement of funds is illustrated in Figure 2.

Using the Traditional Banking System

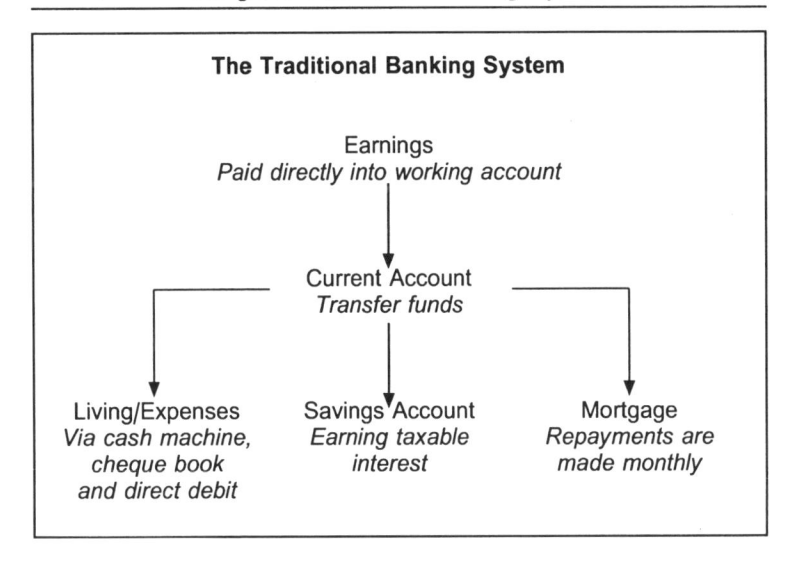

```
┌─────────────────────────────────────────────────────────┐
│              The Traditional Banking System             │
│                                                         │
│                       Earnings                          │
│           Paid directly into working account            │
│                          │                              │
│                          ▼                              │
│                   Current Account                       │
│                    Transfer funds                       │
│           ┌──────────────┼──────────────┐               │
│           ▼              ▼              ▼               │
│    Living/Expenses  Savings Account   Mortgage          │
│    Via cash machine, Earning taxable  Repayments are    │
│       cheque book      interest       made monthly     │
│    and direct debit                                     │
└─────────────────────────────────────────────────────────┘
```

Fig. 2. The traditional banking system flowchart.

Why the traditional banking system costs you time and money

- Money in cheque accounts generally attracts fees and charges.

- Interest *earned* in a savings account is low. At the time of writing this book, you may only receive on average between 5 and 6 per cent, depending on the savings account you have. After tax is taken out you may only receive between 3 and 4 per cent.

- Money used to pay off the mortgage is gobbled up by interest.

- Various accounts can be inconvenient and difficult to balance.

In this book mortgage loans that utilise the traditional banking system are referred to as a **traditional mortgage**. Chapter 4 looks at the most common traditional mortgage products on the market. Chapter 5 will show you how you can reduce both the term and interest payable on a traditional mortgage.

CALCULATING THE COST OF THE TRADITIONAL BANKING SYSTEM

When you add up the cost of interest and charges you repay on a mortgage, in addition to income tax on earnings, it doesn't leave you with much left over. Let's take a closer look at the effect of interest and tax on an average couple's yearly income (see Figure 3). This example is based on a couple with a combined gross yearly income of £27,500.00. They have a standard capital repayment mortgage with a capital balance of £60,000.00. The interest rate is 9.50 per cent over a 25-year term. Their monthly repayments are £524.22 gross of MIRAS.

Combined gross yearly income		£27,500.00
Less combined yearly income tax	£3,943.80	
Less combined National Insurance contributions	£2,234.16	
Total combined net yearly income 'after tax and National Insurance'		£21,322.04
Less total mortgage interest charges for twelve months	£5,727.27	
Add back MIRAS interest subsidy		£429.55
Total combined yearly disposable income net of income tax, national insurance and mortgage interest charges for a twelve-month period – 'the amount left over'		£16,024.32

Fig. 3. The cost of interest and tax on your income.

This is a fair example of where a good majority of many people's hard-earned income goes each year. Having earned a combined gross yearly income of £27,500.00, this couple are left with only £16,024.32 after tax, National Insurance and interest charges have been deducted. The government does, however, provide the mortgage interest relief subsidy (MIRAS) for now, although this may change in the future. Fortunately there is a lot that can be done to reduce the yearly mortgage interest bill, regardless of whether MIRAS is available or not. Chapter 5 looks at the various traditional mortgage reduction methods. Later in this book we will discuss the new flexible mortgage loans and how they can reduce your interest charges by dramatic proportions.

CASE STUDIES

Natalie is well aware

Having had a mortgage for some time now with a number of accounts running, Natalie knows all too well how much the traditional banking system and the mortgage costs her. By finding the right mortgage which will enable her to pay off the capital rapidly, she will save a lot in interest charges. She is a very busy person managing her business affairs and her personal affairs. With this in mind, Natalie would like to look for alternatives to the traditional banking system in order to reduce the time spent managing various accounts. She would also like to reduce the fees and charges she pays on cheque accounts and overdrafts.

John wishes he had done something earlier

Like most people, John paid his mortgage each month, received the statements and accepted this as the way it was. Having already lost an enormous amount of money over past years, he now knows all too well how much a mortgage can cost. John will take his time selecting the new mortgage, ensuring it will be flexible enough to repay as quickly as possible before he retires. John is comfortable using the traditional banking system, but is now more aware of how much it costs. With hindsight, John realises that had he done something earlier, he could be paying his second or third home off with the money he would have saved over the years.

Ross gets a good lesson early

Being a first-time home buyer, Ross was not aware of the amount of money a mortgage will cost him over the course of his life. Like many people, Ross naïvely thought that all mortgage loans were calculated the same way. With his new insight, Ross is now more aware of how much a mortgage could cost him. He will now be very careful to choose the right mortgage. Although it may cost him a little more initially, Ross knows the faster he repays the mortgage, the more money will be saved. Learning this small lesson early has potentially saved Ross thousands over the course of his life.

QUESTIONS AND ANSWERS

The traditional banking system seems to be very one sided and can cost a customer a lot of money. Are there any other ways of banking that are more beneficial for the customer?

Yes, Chapter 6, Profiting from a flexible mortgage, explains how new mortgage loans that utilise the new way of banking can dramatically reduce the amount of money a financial institution can earn.

If a mortgage and the traditional banking system cost people so much of their hard-earned money, why don't more people do something about it?

For the majority of people buying a home and getting a mortgage is seen to be a natural progression in life, like finishing school and going to work. Most people are simply grateful that the financial institution loaned the money to them so they could purchase their dream home. A financial institution is a business like all others and the borrower is the customer. Being the paying customer, you can demand service, negotiate terms and have them delivered at the right price. All too often we treat the financial institution as if they are doing us the favour. It's funny when you consider the level of service you receive at large fast food stores, even if you only spend a minuscule amount of money. Yet you may take for granted having to pay your bank thousands of pounds over a year and still getting the usual low standard of service. Many financial institutions are rigid and inflexible and this usually filters through to their staff. How can you negotiate with a business, if their staff can't help you or are powerless to try? The answer is simple – rather than accept this as the way it is, you can demand what you want or take your business elsewhere.

PERSONAL MORTGAGE AUDIT

- If you have a mortgage at present look at your last mortgage statement. How much interest did you pay in the last month? If you have a capital repayment mortgage, how much capital was repaid?

- How long do you have until your mortgage is repaid? How much interest will you pay over this term?

- If you have an interest-only mortgage, how long do you have until the capital is due to be repaid? How much interest, savings plan or investment premiums and life insurance premiums will you pay back over this term?

- Do you have a separate savings account? How much interest are you earning from this account after tax and charges?

4
Uncovering Traditional Mortgage Loans

All our lives we are putting pennies – our golden pennies – into penny-in-the-slot machines that are empty.

Lorgan Pearsall Smith

This chapter covers the most commonly used traditional mortgage loans in the United Kingdom. As discussed in Chapter 2, there are basically two traditional mortgage types, distinguished by their repayment methods, namely:

- capital repayment
- interest-only repayment.

There can, however, be many variations on these two themes. Each lender may name or tag their mortgage according to a particular feature or benefit of the mortgage. An example is the PEP mortgage. This mortgage is in fact an interest-only mortgage which is linked to a savings plan known as a personal equity plan. By the end of this chapter you will:

- understand the two repayment methods offered by lenders
- decide whether these traditional mortgage loans will suit your present and future requirements
- know the advantages and disadvantages of the traditional mortgage loans.

THE STANDARD CAPITAL REPAYMENT MORTGAGE

This mortgage requires the borrower to make regular monthly repayments. Each repayment pays off a portion of the capital and also the monthly interest charge. Therefore, as each repayment is made the capital is slowly reduced. As the capital owing reduces, less interest is charged, until the mortgage is finally paid in full. This type of mortgage is also referred to as a 'principal and interest' mortgage. Figure 4 illustrates how the capital is gradually reduced over a 25-year term. This graph is based on a capital repayment mortgage with a capital balance of £120,000.00. The interest rate is 9.50 per cent per annum and the monthly repayment is £1,048.44 gross.

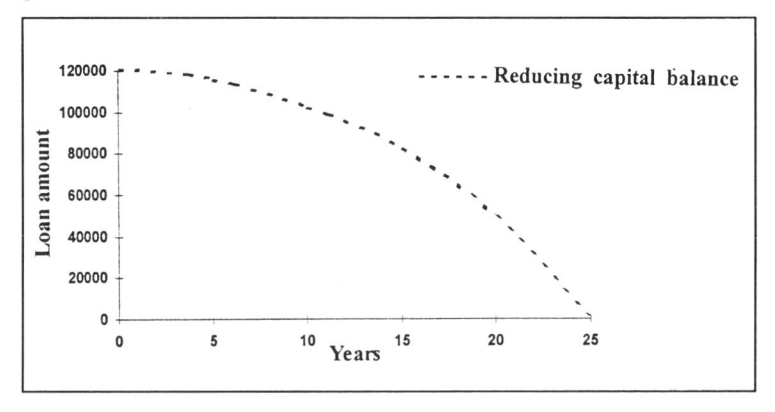

Fig. 4. Traditional capital repayment mortgage graph.

In the example above you would pay back total repayments of £314,532.00, of which £194,532.00 is paid in interest. Lenders may restrict the repayment frequency and also the amount that can be repaid over and above the contractual monthly repayment. These restrictions can make the standard capital repayment mortgage quite expensive and inflexible. Chapter 6 (Profiting from a flexible mortgage) explains the new capital repayment mortgage loans that provide outstanding flexibility and savings.

Many building societies have calculated and charged the interest yearly on a capital repayment mortgage. As discussed in previous chapters, this form of interest calculation and charging method is totally unsatisfactory. The best interest calculation and charging method for a capital repayment mortgage is daily reducible calculation with monthly or quarterly in arrears interest charging method. To benefit from this interest calculation and charging method there must be:

1. no limits on the amount you can repay
2. no limitations on the frequency of the payments
3. no partial or early redemption penalties.

Advantages
- The mortgage is guaranteed to be repaid over time, so long as all the repayments are made.
- There is no requirement for a savings plan or investment to repay the capital of the mortgage.
- The borrower does not have to worry whether an investment or savings plan will perform well.

Disadvantages
- Separate life insurance is usually required.
- The majority of standard capital repayment mortgages are not portable. That is, every time you move house you will have to start a new mortgage.
- They are not flexible to suit borrowers' changing lifestyles.
- Full and partial redemption penalties may apply.
- The frequency of the repayments and overpayments may be restricted.

THE INTEREST-ONLY MORTGAGE

Over past years the interest-only mortgage has become very popular in the United Kingdom. An interest-only mortgage, as the name suggests, requires the borrower to pay the interest charges only. None of the monthly payment repays the capital. Consequently the capital does not reduce during the term, but is repaid at the end of the mortgage agreement. A handful of lenders do allow capital reduction, yet they will usually impose partial redemption penalties and limit the frequency of these capital payments. For the majority of interest-only mortgages the capital will not reduce and will remain static. Consequently the interest calculation and charging method will not affect the amount of interest repaid.

In addition to the monthly interest repayment, the borrower will usually make payments into a separate investment or savings plan. This is used to repay the capital when the mortgage term expires. The most common investments and savings plans used are a personal equity plan 'PEP', a pension or an endowment policy. The lender providing a borrower with an interest-only mortgage will effectively earn maximum interest charges, as the capital may never reduce. The lender may also receive commissions by providing the investment or savings plan to the borrower.

Advantage
- Monthly repayments may be slightly lower than a capital repayment mortgage.

Disadvantages
- There is no capital reduction when each monthly repayment is made.
- A separate savings plan or investment is required to repay the capital when the mortgage term expires. These various savings plans and investments are not guaranteed to provide sufficient returns to repay the mortgage capital.
- A separate life insurance policy may have to be taken out.

UTILISING AN ENDOWMENT POLICY

Since the 1980s the endowment policy has been the most widely used investment for mortgage capital repayment. Generally endowment policies will have a life insurance component. This life cover will usually terminate once the investment has matured. There are a number of endowment policies on the market today. We will cover the most frequently used policies.

With profits endowment
An investor pays the monthly premiums. These premiums are then pooled together with the funds from many other investors and invested. The life company then allocates bonuses to the investors annually. Once these bonuses have been awarded they cannot be taken away, even if the stock market crashes. At the end of the policy term the investors then receive a one-off terminal bonus. This terminal bonus may represent around 50 per cent of the final payment depending upon the investment performance.

Unit linked endowment
The investor's monthly premiums buy units in stock market investments. The unit values can rise and can also fall depending upon the performance of the investments and the market itself. This type of investment can provide a higher rate of return, but it can also have a greater risk of a lower return. An investor can, however, choose to have their monthly premiums invested in a managed fund, which reduces the risk element should the stock market crash. When the investment matures it should provide a tax free lump sum to pay off the mortgage, but this is not guaranteed.

Unit linked with profits endowment
These endowment policies provide the features and benefits of both the unit linked and with profits endowment. The investor's monthly premiums buy units in investments. Bonuses are then subsequently awarded based on the performance of these investments. Once again no guarantees are given that the investment will provide an adequate lump sum large enough to repay the mortgage.

Advantages
- Endowment policies have built-in life policies.//
- There is a potential for a tax free lump sum at policy maturity.
- Possible early repayment of the mortgage.

Disadvantages
- The endowment policy value at maturity may not provide sufficient funds to repay the capital when the mortgage term expires.
- There is no guarantee on the endowment policy's performance.
- The policy holder may have to increase the endowment premiums to ensure the policy value at maturity will cover the mortgage payout.
- Cancelling an endowment policy early may provide little or no returns.

Surrendering an endowment policy
Endowments are long-term investments and the initial set-up costs can be quite expensive. Most financial advisers will not recommend surrendering a policy, but nevertheless 70 per cent of all life insurance policies are cashed in early. People surrender life policies for many different reasons. Some may surrender the policy because they cannot afford the premiums, others just need the additional money. If the endowment policy was taken out prior to 1984, there may be tax relief on the premiums. By surrendering the policy you may lose this benefit.

Selling an endowment policy
Rather than surrendering an endowment policy, many companies now provide other options such as selling or auctioning an endowment policy. You may get a lot more for the policy this way rather than by just cashing it in.

Borrowing against an endowment policy
Rather than surrendering or selling an endowment policy for some spare cash, it may be possible to borrow against it. This allows the policy to remain intact and you will not lose the premiums you have paid into it.

Suspending and reducing payments
If you cannot afford to make the monthly premiums because of changes in your personal circumstances, it may be possible to suspend or reduce the monthly premiums enabling you to keep the policy intact.

UTILISING A PERSONAL EQUITY PLAN

'PEP' is an acronym for 'personal equity plan'. These particular investments can be directly linked to the stock market. As a result they can have a high risk element but may also provide a high return to an investor. A PEP can be more flexible than an endowment policy and it is also tax free. The investment return on a PEP is not guaranteed. Usually a separate life insurance policy has to be taken out, although there are some lenders that offer a PEP mortgage with life cover included as a package deal. The government is presently looking at replacing PEPs with a new savings scheme by April 1999, so they will not be available in the near future.

Advantages
- Personal equity plans are tax efficient.
- It may be possible to pay off the mortgage early should the investments perform well.
- There is a possibility of a lump sum surplus left over after the mortgage has been repaid.

Disadvantages
- Generally a separate life insurance policy has to be taken out.
- A PEP is not guaranteed to provide sufficient returns to repay the mortgage.
- The tax benefits may change and are also not guaranteed.
- The government is looking to replace the PEP with an individual savings account by April 1999. Therefore the PEP will not be available in the near future.

- A PEP can have a higher risk of a lower return if the investments are linked to the stock market.

THE INDIVIDUAL SAVINGS ACCOUNT (ISA)

As discussed previously, the individual savings plan (ISA) is set to replace personal equity plans in April 1999. At the time of writing, only government proposals are available. The ISA proposals set down by the government so far are as follows:

- ISAs can consist of cash, stocks and shares, life insurance and National Savings. Investors will be able to choose which combination of these components to invest, up to a maximum of £7,000.00 for the first tax year (1999/2000), and £5,000.00 per annum thereafter.

- So long as the £5,000.00 limit is not exceeded each year, savers can invest up to £1,000.00 in cash, £1,000.00 in life assurance, and up to £5,000.00 in stocks and shares.

- Like PEPs and Tessas, the investor will be entitled to exemption from income and capital gains tax on these investments.

- Should a Tessa investment mature, the investor can then transfer the capital into a ISA, in addition to their £5,000.00 annual limit.

- To ensure ISAs are highly accessible, they could be used like swipe cards and run through department store checkouts, in addition to traditional channels.

Although these are only proposals, it is clear that ISAs will be very flexible.

UTILISING A PENSION

Primarily a portion of a personal pension fund is used to repay the mortgage capital up to 40 years later. Pensions can provide greater returns than the endowment policy and they are also subject to good tax benefits. The personal pension is more flexible than an endowment policy. With a 'pension mortgage' you make three separate monthly payments, comprised of:

1. a payment for the interest on the mortgage
2. a payment for the pension
3. a payment for the life insurance policy.

Personal pensions were designed specifically to provide a retirement fund and were not designed to be a mortgage reduction vehicle. A pension should not be used for anything other than what it was designed to do, namely provide an income for future years.

Advantage
- Pensions are tax efficient and you will get tax relief on the contributions at the highest rate of income tax that you pay.

Disadvantages
- This scheme uses part of the retirement fund to repay the mortgage and may significantly reduce an individual's future income.
- Up to 25 per cent of the retirement fund can be taken as a tax free lump sum, while the rest must go to providing a retirement annuity. Therefore a large majority of the tax benefit a pension provides may be used on the portion of the pension used to repay the mortgage, rather than utilising the tax benefits on the retirement fund portion.
- The borrower has to take out a separate life insurance policy.

EXAMINING MORTGAGE INCENTIVES

When a lender markets a mortgage to the public they are no different from a car dealer or a supermarket. Lenders add value to their range of products by providing discounts and incentives. Unfortunately there are no free lunches in the world today. A mortgage that may appear to be a bargain initially may end up costing you a lot more in the long run. As competition between lenders increases or if the mortgage market is down, you will notice more incentive schemes being offered. Subsequently when the mortgage market is good you will see less incentives being offered. There are many mortgage incentive schemes offered by lenders today and we will cover the most common.

Cash back offers
Many lenders will offer cash back offers to induce potential

customers into taking their particular mortgage. These cash back offers may be a one-off sum at mortgage application, or the lender may refund anything up to £20,000.00 during the loan term. As mentioned earlier, there are no free lunches and a lender may charge the borrower anything from 0.5 to 0.75 per cent above the standard variable rate, to allow for the costs associated with the cash back. Mortgage redemption penalties usually apply to these incentive schemes. Should a borrower pay off a mortgage early which is subject to a cash back offer, the lender may then require the borrower to repay the cash back payments made.

Free services
Lenders may offer a borrower free services such as no application or legal fees for the initial establishment of the mortgage. It may seem like a good deal initially if money is a little tight. However, the lender may absorb these costs into the interest rate and consequently the rate might be slightly higher. A small saving initially may cost the borrower a lot more over the mortgage term.

Combination incentives
Lenders may offer a combination of cash back and subsidised fees. Once again these incentives may be absorbed into other fees and charges of the mortgage.

AVOIDING TIES AND COMPULSORIES

Ties and compulsories usually relate to any insurance product a borrower must take out with the lender in conjunction with a package deal. These ties and compulsories generally form part of the package deal's terms and conditions. Compulsory insurance products earn the lender additional income and without this additional income, the lender could not afford to offer such a competitive deal.

As discussed in Chapter 2 (Considering mortgage protection insurance), a borrower can choose any insurance product they wish and can use any company they want to use. However, when a lender offers a package deal, they may insist the borrower use their own insurance products or services. If the borrower refuses to take these insurance products or services, the lender may then decline the package deal offered. Package deals will generally provide minimal savings and in some cases they may end up costing the borrower a lot more over the course of the mortgage.

CASE STUDIES

Natalie chooses to shop around
Natalie currently has an interest-only mortgage but would like to change to a capital repayment mortgage, enabling her to pay the capital down faster. Although she will refinance the interest-only mortgage to a capital repayment mortgage, Natalie will continue to pay the monthly PEP premiums. Once the PEP has matured, she will use these funds as a deposit on an investment property. Natalie is concerned that the traditional standard capital repayment mortgage will not be flexible enough and may not suit her needs adequately. She will continue looking for a capital repayment mortgage that will provide the flexibility she wants. Being an astute businesswoman she is already wary of incentive schemes, ties and compulsories.

John makes his decision
John already has an interest-only mortgage which is linked to an endowment policy, but he is not satisfied with it. He has decided to remortgage it to a capital repayment mortgage. John would also like to keep the endowment policy going, without reducing the premium amounts. John is not overly happy with the limitations and restrictions of a standard capital repayment mortgage, so he will look around for something more flexible.

Ross makes a quick decision
Having examined the two repayment methods, Ross quickly decided on a capital repayment mortgage. He chose capital repayment for the safety of knowing that the capital will be repaid once all the repayments are made. As Ross's wife is pregnant, the standard capital repayment mortgage may not provide the flexibility they will need during this difficult period. Ross likes the idea of finding a lender that may waive the initial set-up costs, as their deposit is minimal and their cash situation is tight.

QUESTIONS AND ANSWERS

Is it worth selling or cashing in an endowment policy?

No, all financial advisers should advise against doing this. It is important to be wary of advisers who may advise you to cash it in, or sell it and invest the proceeds into another investment. The decision to cash in or sell an endowment policy short term because of financial pressures may result in you receiving little or no return. As discussed earlier in this chapter, a wise decision would be to suspend or reduce monthly payments to the endowment policy if this is allowed. Another alternative could be to borrow against the endowment policy itself. The decision you make is ultimately yours, so make the decision with due care.

Will I pay more interest on a capital repayment mortgage than an interest-only mortgage?

No, you will always pay less interest with a capital repayment mortgage if the comparison between the two mortgage types is based on the same amount borrowed, same rate and term.

How can I tell whether a mortgage incentive is genuine?

It's very hard to determine whether a mortgage incentive will actually save you money. At the end of the day the lender has to recover the costs of any give-aways. The cost of incentives offered such as up to £20,000.00 cash back has to be found from somewhere and it is usually the borrower who will pay for it in the long run.

PERSONAL MORTGAGE AUDIT

- What type of mortgage do you have at present or are you considering: capital repayment or interest-only?

- Which repayment method would best suit your present and future needs?

- If you have an interest-only mortgage or are considering one, which savings plan or investment are you using or considering?

- Are these traditional mortgage loans flexible enough for your particular circumstances?

5
Utilising Traditional Mortgage Reduction Methods

> Time is money!
> *Benjamin Franklin*

In this chapter we will look at the various ways in which you can reduce the term of a capital repayment and interest-only mortgage. The various reduction methods have been labelled 'traditional', as they utilise the traditional way of banking (see Chapter 3). As discussed in Chapter 3, interest and fees can cost people an enormous amount of their hard-earned money. These various reduction methods can provide you with substantial savings.

The following mortgage reduction methods apply predominantly to a capital repayment mortgage. These reduction methods are based on the capital repayment mortgage having interest calculated daily, charged either monthly or quarterly in arrears. The way an interest-only mortgage can be reduced is limited, as many lenders may restrict capital reduction payments, limit repayment frequency and may also impose redemption penalties during the term of the mortgage. Taking this into consideration, we will look at other alternatives including the various savings plans and investments used to repay an interest-only mortgage.

INCREASING YOUR DEPOSIT

When a mortgage is first established it may benefit you to increase the amount of deposit you are thinking about paying. When more deposit is paid, less money is then borrowed. As the amount borrowed is less, less interest is subsequently charged. By increasing your deposit when the mortgage is established you can greatly reduce:

- the monthly repayment
- the interest charges payable

- the mortgage indemnity guarantee premium (MIG)
- the scheduled repayment term.

Reducing the monthly repayment
By increasing the initial deposit paid, the amount borrowed on a **capital repayment** mortgage will subsequently be less. As a result the monthly **repayment** will reduce. Should the mortgage be **interest-only**, by paying more deposit you will reduce the amount borrowed, subsequently the monthly **interest charges** will be less.

Reducing interest charges payable
Obviously the less money you borrow the less interest will be charged, regardless of whether it is an interest-only mortgage or a capital repayment mortgage.

Reducing MIG premiums
As discussed in Chapter 2, MIG premiums and fees are calculated on the **loan to value ratio** (LTV) and the **amount borrowed**. The higher the LTV ratio and the higher the amount borrowed, the higher the premiums. By paying more deposit you will lower the LTV ratio and also the amount borrowed. This will reduce the MIG premiums charged. A large percentage of lenders charge the borrower MIG starting at 75 per cent of LTV ratio. For example, if the LTV ratio is 77 per cent, then it may benefit you to pay the difference in deposit and reduce the LTV ratio below the 75 per cent threshold. As a result you will not be charged a MIG premium.

Reducing the scheduled repayment term
This is for capital repayment mortgages only. By paying a larger deposit you can reduce the monthly repayments. Rather than reducing the monthly repayments, you could reduce the term of the mortgage and keep the repayments the same as they would have been prior to paying the larger deposit. For example, if you were initially going to borrow £60,000.00 over a term of 20 years, your monthly repayments may be £579.00. By paying an extra £2,000.00 deposit, the amount borrowed would reduce to £58,000.00 and your repayments over the 20-year term would reduce to £559.71 per month. Rather than having lower monthly repayments, if you kept the repayments to the original £579.00, the term would then reduce to 18 years.

REDUCING THE TERM OF A MORTGAGE

Traditionally mortgages have been taken out over a term of either 20 or 25 years. Although the majority of lenders work in round figures, it is possible to choose any term that suits you, such as 17-, 21- or 23-year time periods. When you reduce the scheduled repayment term of a **capital repayment mortgage**, the monthly repayments will increase. However, with an **interest-only mortgage** the term makes no difference to the monthly interest repayment.

By reducing the term of a £100,000.00 **capital repayment mortgage**, with interest charged at 7 per cent, from 25 years to 20 years, you will reduce the interest charges by approximately £25,962.00 and only increase the monthly repayment by approximately £68.52 per month.

> **Important: before you decide to reduce the mortgage term, you should make sure that if interest rates rose dramatically, you would be able to afford the higher monthly repayments.**

MAKING YOUR PAYMENTS FORTNIGHTLY

If your mortgage interest is calculated daily one of the most successful ways to reduce the term of a capital repayment mortgage is to make fortnightly repayments rather than standard monthly repayments. By paying fortnightly you will reduce the mortgage balance twice in one month, rather than just the once. Interest is then calculated on this reduced balance resulting in less interest being charged. The other main reason why fortnightly repayments reduce the mortgage term so well is that there are 26 fortnights in a calendar year. By paying fortnightly you actually make one additional monthly payment per year. Let's take a closer look:

Example: Your monthly repayments are £1,048.44 per month, over 25 years, based on an amount borrowed of £120,000.00 at 9.50 per cent per annum. To calculate your total yearly payments paid fortnightly, you would divide your monthly repayments in half and multiply these by 26 fortnights.

That is: £1,048.44 divided by 2, multiplied by 26 fortnights = £13,629.72.

Subtracting your total yearly instalments *paid fortnightly*, i.e. £13,629.72, from the total yearly instalments *paid monthly*, i.e. £12,581.28, the difference between the two would then be:

$$£13,629.72 - £12,581.28 = £1,048.44$$

So by paying fortnightly you are in effect making one extra contractual payment per year off the mortgage. (See Figure 5.)

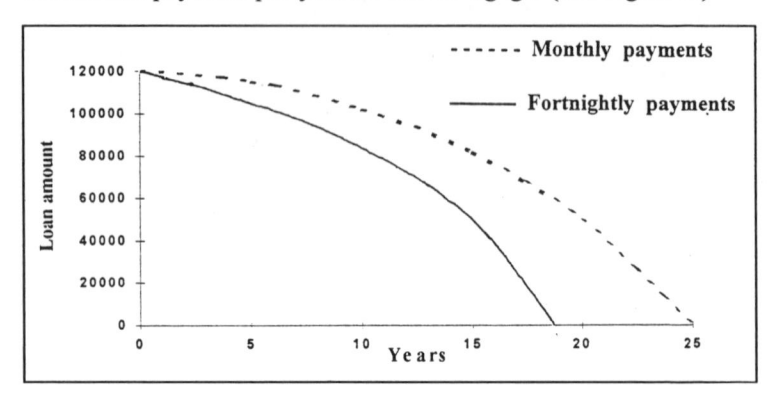

Fig. 5. Comparison between monthly and fortnightly repayments.

In this example, by simply paying your payments fortnightly rather than monthly, you could reduce your mortgage from 25 years to 18.75 years. Paying fortnightly is an easy way of reducing a capital repayment mortgage term and subsequently reducing the interest charges payable.

MAKING YOUR PAYMENTS WEEKLY

This is quite a demanding way to pay your mortgage. For those of you who thought paying weekly would compound the fortnightly scenario, I have some bad news for you. Paying weekly does not have as significant an effect on the mortgage term as fortnightly payments. Of course, you may save an extra month over fortnightly payments as a result of your paying down the mortgage balance weekly. However, the main reason paying fortnightly works is that there are 52 weeks in a year and 26 fortnights in a year. This in effect means that, whether fortnightly or weekly, you can only make one extra full repayment per year.

Let's look at this a little closer

In the previous example, your monthly contractual payment was £1,048.44 per month. To arrive at weekly payments you would divide the monthly payment by four and then multiply it by 52 (= weeks in a year):

£1,048.44 divided by 4, multiplied by 52 weeks = £13,629.72

As you can see the total payable per year, paid weekly, is the same as paying fortnightly!

INCREASING YOUR REPAYMENT

By increasing the amount of your repayments you reduce the capital faster. Consequently as the capital reduces, less interest is charged and a larger portion of the repayment is used to reduce the capital. Unfortunately many people are restricted in the amount of extra money they can afford to pay over and above the minimum monthly repayment amount. Unless the mortgage has a redraw facility – that is, in laymen's terms, 'access to the overpayments', such overpayments may be hard to access should an emergency arise.

The table in Figure 6 assumes a capital repayment mortgage, with a capital balance of £70,000.00, at an interest rate of 8.95 per cent.

Percentage payment increased	Total monthly repayment	Repayment term	Total amount payable	Total interest payable	Total savings
	£		£	£	£
0%	585.04	25 years 0 months	175,512.00	105,512.00	nil
5%	614.29	21 years 3 months	156,643.95	86,643.95	18,868.05
10%	643.54	18 years 8 months	144,152.96	74,152.96	31,359.04
15%	672.79	16 years 9 months	135,230.79	65,230.79	40,281.21
20%	702.04	15 years 3 months	128,473.32	58,473.32	47,038.68
25%	731.30	14 years 0 months	122,858.40	52,858.40	52,653.60
30%	760.55	13 years 0 months	118,645.80	48,645.80	56,866.20
35%	789.80	12 years 1 month	114,521.00	44,521.00	60,991.00
40%	819.05	11 years 4 months	111,390.80	41,390.80	64,121.20
45%	848.30	10 years 8 months	108,502.40	38,582.40	66,929.60
50%	877.56	10 years 1 month	106,184.76	36,184.76	69,327.24

Fig. 6. The effect of increasing the monthly repayment.

The monthly repayments are £585.04 gross of MIRAS. This table clearly illustrates the interest savings that can be achieved by increasing the monthly repayment.

You can dramatically improve the savings illustrated in Figure 6 by paying your repayments fortnightly. If you increased the monthly repayment by 15 per cent making it £672.79, by paying half this amount every fortnight, you would reduce the term to only 10 years and 2 months, saving you a further £28,200.83. Although Figure 6 above illustrates the effect of increasing your repayment by up to 50 per cent, this in most cases may not be possible. However, increasing your monthly repayment by a small amount, coupled with making the repayments fortnightly, will result in dramatic savings.

MAKING LUMP SUM PAYMENTS

By making a lump sum payment you effectively reduce the capital of the mortgage. The interest is then calculated on this reduced balance and the interest charged will be less. Consequently as less interest is charged more of the monthly repayment is used to repay the capital. Lump sum payments dramatically reduce the overall term of a mortgage.

It must be noted that unless the mortgage has a redraw facility, it may be hard to access these overpayments should an emergency arise. There are some mortgage loans on the market that have redraw facilities, allowing the borrower free access to any overpayments (see Chapter 6, Profiting from a flexible mortgage). Let's look at the example below to see what effect a lump sum payment can make:

Example: If you made a lump sum payment of £5,000.00 and continued to make your standard monthly repayment, what effect would this have?

Assuming a loan amount of £120,000.00 over a 25-year term at 9.50 per cent per annum, the monthly repayments would be £1,048.44 gross. Paying a lump sum amount of £5,000.00 would reduce the mortgage balance to £115,000.00. As a result of this lump sum payment, the term of the mortgage would be reduced to approximately 21 years and 7 months. If we took this a stage further and paid the monthly repayments fortnightly rather than monthly, the term would reduce by a further 3 years and 8 months, to only 17 years and 11 months.

CONSOLIDATING YOUR DEBTS

Consolidating debts can have major benefits and may save you a lot of money in interest charges. Unfortunately this form of reduction method is restricted to those people who have adequate equity in their property. To illustrate the benefits of consolidating debts into one, we will assume the borrower has the following debts:

1. A capital repayment mortgage of £50,000.00, secured on a property worth £120,000.00. The interest rate is 7.50 per cent per annum over a term of 20 years. The monthly repayments are £402.80 gross of MIRAS and the total amount payable over this term would amount to £96,671.18.
2. A car loan of £15,000.00 with interest charged at 10 per cent over five years. The monthly repayments are £375.00 per month and the total amount payable over this term would be £22,500.00.
3. A personal loan of £5,000.00 with interest charged at 11 per cent over three years. The monthly repayments are £184.72 per month and the total amount payable over this term would be £6,650.00.

Combined monthly debts:

	Balance £	*Interest payable* £	*Total payable* £	*Repayments* £
Mortgage	50,000.00	46,671.18	96,671.18	402.80
Car loan	15,000.00	7,500.00	22,500.00	375.00
Personal loan	5,000.00	1,650.00	6,650.00	184.72
TOTAL	70,000.00	55,821.18	125,821.18	962.52

When consolidating together, the total debts would amount to £70,000.00. If you took out a mortgage of £70,000.00 secured against the property valued at £120,000.00, the loan to value ratio (LTV) would be 58 per cent, so MIG premiums would not be charged (see Chapter 2, Mortgage indemnity guarantee premiums). We will assume that the same mortgage rate of 7.50 per cent per annum applies. By slightly reducing the term to 17 years the new monthly repayment gross of MIRAS would be £608.10. The total amount payable over this term would be £124,051.70. By paying half the repayment of £608.10 fortnightly, you would reduce the term down to approximately 14.5 years.

If, however, you continued to pay the combined monthly payments prior to consolidating of £962.52, this would then reduce the mortgage term down to approximately 8 years. Taking the example further, if you made fortnightly payments rather than monthly, this would reduce the term down to just over 7 years and the total amount you would pay back would be approximately £91,760.00, providing you with a saving of approximately £34,061.00 in interest charges. The only *disadvantage* of consolidating your debts together would be if you paid the minimum monthly repayment of £608.10. The only real saving you would then achieve would be the difference between what you were paying prior to the consolidation i.e. £962.52, and the new monthly repayment of £608.10.

SPLITTING A MORTGAGE

Some lenders now allow a borrower to construct their own mortgage by mixing and matching various mortgage types into one. This type of mortgage is referred to as a **cocktail loan**. An example would be if you had a combined debt of £50,000.00 and you split it into two separate loans. You may choose one portion to be a variable interest rate and the other portion to be a five-year fixed rate.

Example: £25,000.00   /   £25,000.00
               (5-year fixed)   (variable)

By splitting a mortgage you effectively spread the risk. So, should interest rates rise dramatically, a portion will be fixed, and if interest rates fall, you could also enjoy the lower rates. As described in previous chapters, fixed rates will usually attract redemption penalties and the lender may restrict the frequency and amount that can be repaid. Keeping a portion of the mortgage on a variable rate allows you the freedom to make fortnightly repayments, but also pay lump sum payments without being charged any redemption penalties. Some lenders will allow up to five different split combinations and the variety of split combinations can include:

- variable interest rate
- discounted interest rate

- capped interest rate
- fixed interest rate.

The split percentage is not limited to 50/50, and you may wish to fix, say, 75 per cent of the mortgage on a 5-year fixed and the remaining 25 per cent on a variable rate. It will all depend upon what suits your circumstances the best. The majority of lenders that provide cocktail loans generally restrict discounted rates to one portion, although they may allow the borrower to choose as many fixed or variable rates as they wish.

> **It is also possible to have half the mortgage interest-only with an endowment, PEP or pension and the other half capital repayment.**

UTILISING SAVINGS PLANS AND INVESTMENTS

Savings plans and investments can be used to repay the capital of an interest-only mortgage, as discussed in Chapter 4, Uncovering traditional mortgage loans. Many lenders do not allow the borrower to reduce the capital during the term of an interest-only mortgage, or they may limit the amount and also the frequency of the capital payments. If they do allow capital reduction payments they may impose redemption penalties. Therefore many of the reduction methods outlined in this chapter may not be suitable. If you have an interest-only mortgage that has these limitations and restrictions, but would like to pay it off faster, you could:

- increase your savings plan or investment policy monthly premiums
- take out an additional savings plan or investment policy
- refinance to a capital repayment mortgage or flexible mortgage
- refinance to a current account mortgage.

Increasing your monthly premiums

Increasing your monthly contributions to a savings plan or investment policy will increase the value of the savings plan or investment at maturity. As the value grows faster, you may be able to pay the interest-only mortgage off earlier. Unfortunately not everyone can afford to pay extra monthly premiums, so this method is limited.

Taking out an additional savings plan or investment
Rather than leaving surplus money in a low interest savings account, it may pay you to invest this money into a higher yielding investment. Before you decide on an investment or savings plan, you should be absolutely sure of its risk potential. As a rule of thumb, the greater the potential for a large return, the higher the risk. The lower the risk, the greater the potential for a lower return.

You should also make sure you can afford these extra monthly premiums comfortably. The majority of savings plans and investments are long-term commitments, generally between 5 and 10 years. Should you wish to cash these investments in because of an emergency, the amount you receive could be a lot less than you have paid in. When the savings plan or investment you choose matures, these funds can then be used to repay the mortgage capital.

Refinancing to a capital repayment mortgage
If your present interest-only mortgage does not allow capital reduction, or redemption penalties apply, then you could refinance your interest-only mortgage to a capital repayment mortgage. Before you do this, you have to ensure that you can:

- afford to pay the higher capital repayment
- afford to continue paying the investment or savings plans monthly premiums – as discussed earlier, cashing in a savings plan or investment early can result in the investor receiving a lot less than they paid in.

Refinancing to a current account mortgage
Another option for those people who have an interest-only mortgage, but would like to pay the capital off each month, is the current account mortgage (discussed in great detail in the next chapter). A current account mortgage allows the borrower to have their wage paid directly into the mortgage and it can be either interest-only or capital repayment. Even if the borrower doesn't pay anything off the capital each month, the effect of having their wages paid directly into the mortgage reduces the capital outstanding and the interest charged each month will be less. (See Chapter 6, Capitalising on a current account mortgage.)

Utilising Traditional Mortgage Reduction Methods

CASE STUDIES

Natalie reserves judgement

Because Natalie is using all of her savings as a large deposit, this will reduce the amount she has to borrow and her new mortgage will not be subject to any MIG premiums. She likes the idea of paying fortnightly repayments, although she is still looking for something even more flexible. If possible, she would like to have her wages paid directly into the mortgage. Natalie has decided to reserve judgement until she has looked at the current account mortgage.

John sees the light at the end of the tunnel

As John is keeping his endowment policy he cannot afford to pay much more than the standard monthly repayment. However, John has decided to pay them fortnightly. John has an investment policy which matures in six months time, and he will use this as a lump sum payment. This will dramatically reduce the capital owing and will consequently reduce the term of the mortgage.

Ross is excited by his future prospects

Ross felt disillusioned when he realised how much a mortgage could cost him. Having now studied the various mortgage reduction methods, he feels happier with his future prospects. Ross unfortunately cannot afford to pay a larger deposit or extra monthly repayments. He has decided to pay his monthly repayments fortnightly and when his situation changes, will pay a little more with each payment. Ross will continue looking for a mortgage that will provide him with more flexibility than the standard capital repayment mortgage.

QUESTIONS AND ANSWERS

Can you pay fortnightly on an interest-only mortgage?

No, with an interest-only mortgage you generally only repay the interest per month and no capital is repaid until the end of the contract term. If this is the case, it is of no benefit to you making fortnightly repayments to an interest-only mortgage.

If we make lump sum payments to our capital repayment mortgage, how do we access these funds should we need them?

Some capital repayment mortgage loans have redraw facilities.

Redraw facilities are usually limited to a flexible mortgage, although some lenders provide them with a standard capital repayment mortgage. Redraw facilities allow the borrower to access over-payments via a cheque book or debit card (see Chapter 6, Benefiting from a flexible mortgage).

PERSONAL MORTGAGE AUDIT

- If you have a capital repayment mortgage or are considering one, does it allow you to pay as much as you like as often as you like? Do redemption penalties apply ?

- Are you presently or are you considering paying your repayments fortnightly? Could you comfortably afford to pay a little more each fortnight?

- Does your present mortgage or the one you are considering have a redraw facility? Do you have any spare savings that could be used as a lump sum payment to reduce the capital balance?

- If you are considering a mortgage, can you afford to pay a larger deposit?

- Would debt consolidation be of benefit to you? Do you have the discipline to use it to your advantage?

- If you have an interest-only mortgage, what is the estimated pay-out term? Are you happy with this or would you like to reduce this term?

- Could you comfortably afford to increase your savings plan or investment policy monthly premiums?

- Are you presently saving money each month in a low interest savings account? Could this money be put to better use by setting up an additional savings plan or investment?

- Would refinancing your interest-only mortgage to a capital repayment mortgage be of benefit to you? Could you comfortably afford to continue paying your savings plan or investment policy monthly premiums, in addition to the slightly higher capital repayments?

6
Profiting from a Flexible Mortgage

> Succeeding financially is not dependent upon how much money you can earn... it is dependent upon how much money you can save...
>
> *Tony Cornell*

For many people, the certainty of a steady income and a 'job-for-life' is fast disappearing, leading to a general feeling of insecurity about their present and future situations. Buying a house and taking out a mortgage is also often perceived to be riskier than it was in the past. Consequently more people are opting to rent and thus avoid the risks involved in buying a property. Fortunately the lenders have responded and are now providing highly flexible mortgage products that adapt to a borrower's changing lifestyle.

Flexible mortgages are becoming more and more popular within the United Kingdom. They are a mini revolution when compared to the traditional capital repayment and interest-only mortgages. A flexible mortgage allows the borrower freedom to manoeuvre the mortgage when their circumstances change. Surprisingly, flexible mortgages were not designed out of the kindness of the lender's heart, but out of a need to survive in this competitive environment. Unlike the traditional straitjacket mortgages we have discussed in previous chapters, a flexible mortgage can put you in the driver's seat of your financial future, enabling you to work smart not hard.

By the end of this chapter you will:

- understand the benefits of a flexible mortgage over the traditional standard capital repayment and interest-only mortgage

- understand the new way of banking and how it can save you time and money as compared with the traditional way of banking

- understand the difference between a flexible mortgage and a current account mortgage

Working hard not smart.

- decide which flexible mortgage will suit your present and future requirements.

There are many types of flexible mortgage loans on offer today, the most popular being:

- the flexible mortgage
- the current account mortgage.

Many lenders use the term 'flexible' and although a mortgage may be called flexible, it may be no more than a standard capital repayment mortgage which allows for overpayments. Lenders may also set limitations on these overpayments, restricting the amount that can be paid. This chapter will help you to choose the most beneficial flexible mortgage.

BENEFITING FROM A FLEXIBLE MORTGAGE

A flexible mortgage can be either an interest-only or a capital repayment mortgage. The majority of lenders who provide flexible mortgages calculate interest daily and charge it to the mortgage balance either monthly or quarterly in arrears. Many flexible mortgage schemes do not offer discounted rates or cash backs. In addition to this the interest rate may be slightly higher. None the less, a good flexible mortgage when used properly can save people more money than traditional mortgages. A good flexible mortgage will have a host of features that accommodate a borrower's changing lifestyle, such as:

- the ability to make overpayments
- allowing for payment holidays
- allowing for underpayments
- redraw facilities.

Making overpayments

Overpayments allow the borrower to pay amounts over and above the set monthly repayment. A good flexible mortgage allows the borrower to make irregular payments at any time, for any amount, without any redemption penalties charged. By making overpayments you reduce the capital loan balance; consequently the interest calculated on this reduced balance is less.

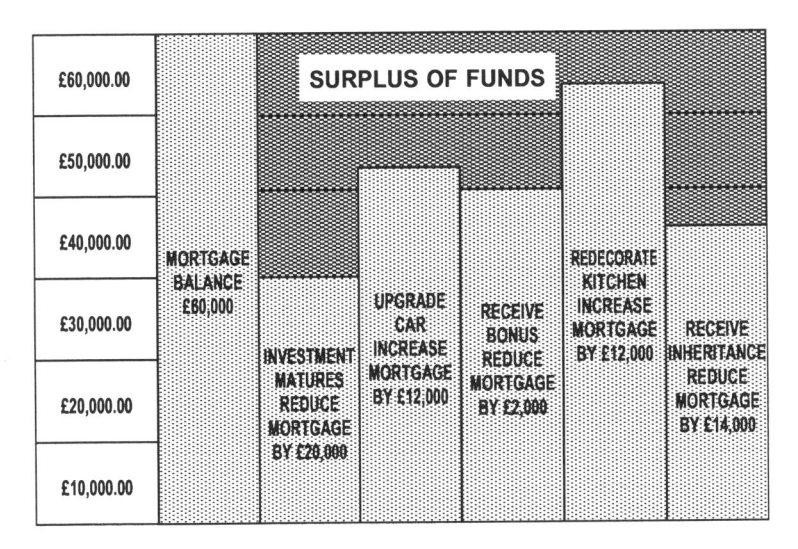

Fig. 7. Creating a surplus of funds.

As you can see from Figure 7, when you pay down the capital balance with overpayments or lump sum payments, a **surplus of funds** is created. These surplus funds can then be used to take payment holidays, redraw funds as you need them and make underpayments.

Reducing your tax
By paying your savings into the mortgage, you reduce the capital balance and therefore reduce the amount of interest charged. Although you would not *earn* any interest on these savings paid into the mortgage, you would *save* interest at the mortgage interest rate. The only difference between *saving* interest and *earning* interest is that **interest earned is taxable** and **interest saved is not**.

Denying the financial institution the benefit of the 'fat'
By paying your savings into your mortgage you effectively deny the financial institutions the **fat** (as discussed in Chapter 3, Understanding the traditional banking system). The 'fat' is the profit difference between what they pay you for the money you invest in savings accounts and the amount they charge you when you borrow money from them.

Redrawing surplus funds
Should the borrower make overpayments they may as a result build up a surplus of funds. These surplus funds may then be accessed via a cheque book, switch card or cash machine debit card. Not all lenders offer a switch card and cash machine debit card for withdrawal of surplus funds. Not having this feature greatly reduces the convenience and flexibility of the mortgage.

Taking a payment holiday
Payment holidays allow the borrower to make no repayments for a month or several. This feature is designed for periods when the borrower cannot afford to make monthly repayments, or would prefer not to. Such periods could be, for example, around Christmas time, or if a baby is born and a little leeway is required. Lenders differ greatly in the payment break duration they will allow and the borrower will generally have to have had the mortgage for 6–9 months before a payment holiday is granted.

Making underpayments
By overpaying the mortgage the borrower subsequently builds up a

Profiting from a Flexible Mortgage

surplus of funds. If the surplus of funds warrants it, the lender may then allow the borrower to make underpayments.

Using the capital repayment method
Like a traditional capital repayment mortgage, a set monthly repayment has to be paid each month. A portion of the monthly repayment pays the interest charges and a portion pays down the capital balance. Unlike many traditional capital repayment mortgages, the majority of lenders calculate the interest daily and charge it monthly or quarterly in arrears. Because the interest is calculated daily, all traditional reduction methods can be used with a flexible mortgage as discussed in Chapter 5. Redemption penalties do not usually apply to a flexible mortgage, so the borrower has complete freedom to pay as much and as often as they like.

Advantages
- Interest calculated daily and charged monthly or quarterly in arrears.
- All traditional reduction methods can be utilised.
- Redemption penalties do not usually apply to a flexible mortgage.
- Limited restrictions on payment amounts and the repayment frequency.
- Surplus funds save interest at the mortgage rate and this is non-taxable.
- Allows for and adapts to a borrower's changing lifestyle.
- Surplus funds can be easily redrawn from the mortgage.

Disadvantages
- Surplus funds are easily accessible and may not suit undisciplined borrowers.
- The interest rate may be slightly higher than a traditional mortgage and discounts and cash back may not apply.

Using the interest-only repayment method
A flexible interest-only mortgage will generally have all the features of the flexible capital repayment mortgage, such as ability to make lump sum payments, payment holidays and so on. The minimum monthly payment is interest only. A good flexible interest-only mortgage allows

the borrower to pay down the capital balance, therefore reducing the monthly interest charges. A savings plan or investment can also be used to repay the capital balance in the future.

Advantages
- Allows the borrower to pay down the capital balance during the term.
- Has all the features of the capital repayment mortgage such as payment holidays, underpayments, etc.
- The borrower can make fortnightly payments, lump sum payments and overpayments to reduce the capital balance.
- The borrower does not have to rely on a savings plan or investment to repay the capital.
- Savings can be paid into the mortgage, saving interest at the mortgage rate, and this is non-taxable.

Disadvantages
- Access to surplus funds may not suit an undisciplined borrower.
- The interest rate may be higher than a traditional interest-only mortgage and discounts and cashback may not apply.

CAPITALISING ON A CURRENT ACCOUNT MORTGAGE

Often regarded as the mortgage of the future, the current account mortgage puts your savings and borrowings together in one-easy-to-manage account. It provides all the facilities of a current account, including a cheque book and switch/debit/cash card, and allows for standing orders and direct debits. In a nutshell your current account mortgage is your savings account, cheque account and mortgage all in one. Like the flexible mortgage, the interest rates may be slightly higher than with traditional mortgages, and discounts and cash back may not apply. However, regardless of this, when used properly a current account mortgage can save you more money than the traditional mortgages. Listed below are some of the many features of a good current account mortgage:

- cheque book, switch card and debit card access
- allows for standing orders and direct debits

Profiting from a Flexible Mortgage

- allows the borrower's wage to be paid directly into the mortgage
- provides monthly statements
- no transaction or account-keeping charges
- 24-hour telephone access.

A current account mortgage allows the borrower to have their earnings paid directly into the mortgage. By paying your income directly into the mortgage you utilise the new way of banking. This has many advantages over the traditional way of banking, as discussed in Chapter 3. Figure 8 illustrates how the new way of banking works.

```
                        Earnings
               Paid directly into mortgage
                           │
                           ▼
                        Mortgage
               Savings stay in mortgage saving
                interest which is non-taxable
                           │
                           ▼
                     Draw expenses
               Via cash machine, switch card,
                  cheque book, direct debit
```

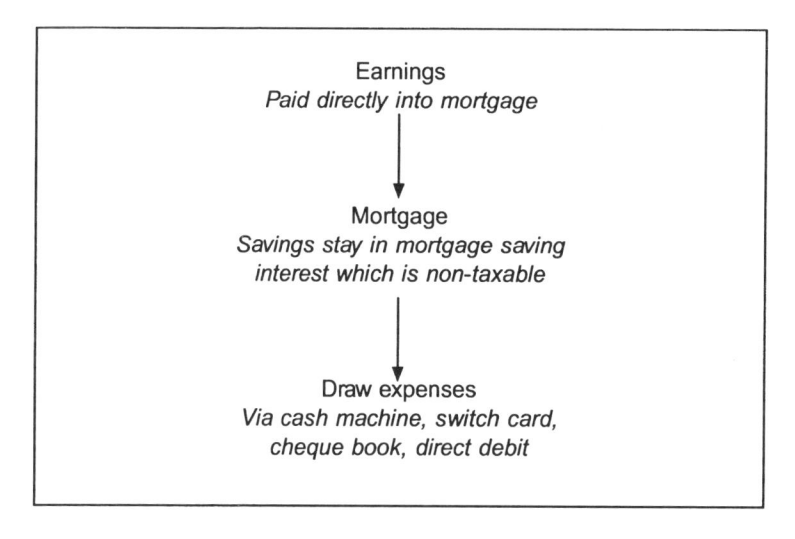

Fig. 8. The new way of banking flowchart.

Paying your earnings directly into the mortgage reduces the capital balance greatly and as a result reduces the amount of interest you will pay. Unfortunately we all have bills to pay each month, so you have complete flexibility to draw on these surplus funds at any time via a switch/debit/cash card and cheque book. Some lenders also provide 24-hour telephone access lines. To help you balance your current account mortgage, the majority of lenders will provide monthly mortgage statements, rather than half-yearly or yearly. Figure 9 shows how a current account mortgage works.

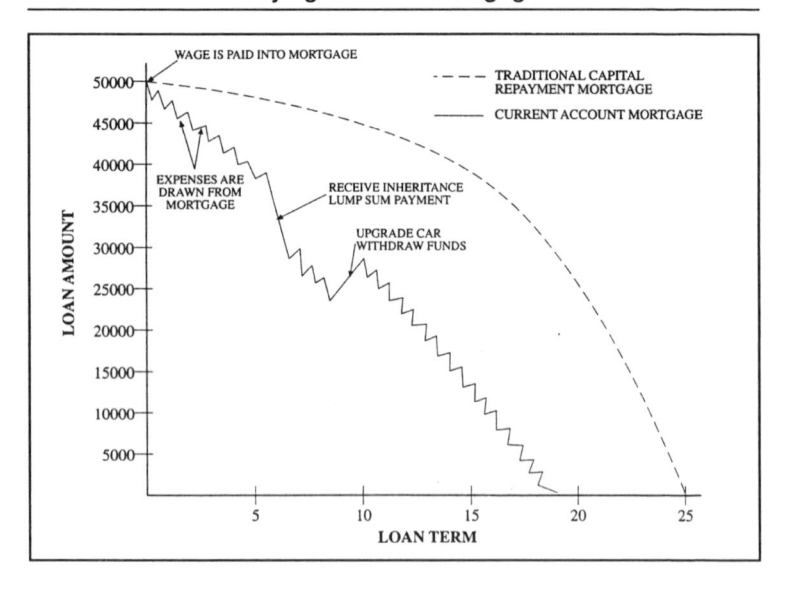

Fig. 9. Utilising a current account mortgage.

In order to illustrate clearly how a current account mortgage works, the graph in Figure 9 is not to scale. As you can see, your wages are paid in each month which reduces the capital balance. The interest calculated on this reduced balance will as a result be less. When funds are drawn from the mortgage to pay for expenses, the capital balance will subsequently increase. Therefore, the longer you leave the funds in the mortgage the greater the interest savings. Using a credit card is a good way of deferring expenditure (explained in more detail later in this chapter).

Transferring any savings you have into your current account mortgage **saves interest** at the mortgage interest rate and these funds will not be subject to taxation. A current account mortgage can save an enormous amount of money when used properly. It denies the financial institutions the 'fat' and reduces the need for multiple accounts, saving you fees and charges. A good current account mortgage should have all the flexible features that a standard flexible mortgage has, such as payment holidays, underpayments, etc.

Utilising a capital repayment current account mortgage

This requires the borrower to make a minimum capital and interest repayment each month. Paying monthly income directly into the mortgage dramatically reduces the interest charges and the term of the mortgage. To illustrate the benefits of this, let's assume a capital balance of £70,000.00, with an interest rate of 8 per cent over a term of 25 years. The minimum monthly repayment gross of MIRAS would be £540.27. The borrower has their net income of £2,000.00 per month paid directly into the mortgage and withdraws £1,200.00 per month to pay monthly expenses. By leaving the difference, i.e. £259.73, in the mortgage, the mortgage will be paid off in approximately 11 years, saving the borrower approximately £54,000.00 in interest charges.

Utilising an interest-only current account mortgage

Most borrowers will have a savings plan, investment or pension plan to repay the interest-only mortgage capital in the future. A current account mortgage enables the borrower to reduce the capital during the term without dramatically increasing their monthly repayments. Paying income directly into the mortgage each month reduces the capital balance and consequently reduces the amount of interest charged.

To highlight the benefit of using an interest-only current account mortgage, let's assume the following: a loan balance of £70,000.00 at 8.00 per cent per annum, resulting in monthly interest charges of £466.66 gross of MIRAS. If the borrower has a net income of £2,000.00 paid directly into the mortgage each month and leaves only £50.00 in the mortgage after expenses and the monthly interest charge are paid, this would reduce the mortgage capital by approximately £31,000.00 after 20 years. If the amount left in the mortgage is increased to £100.00 per month, the mortgage will be completely paid off in approximately 21 years. As you can see, an interest-only current account mortgage can be reduced quite easily, without having to increase dramatically the monthly payments. The investment or savings plan can then be used to reinvest in property or the funds can be used towards the borrower's retirement fund.

UTILISING A CREDIT CARD TO REDUCE INTEREST COSTS

You are probably wondering how a credit card could possibly reduce interest costs, when by all accounts they actually cost you money. A credit card when used properly can save you a considerable amount of money. When income is paid directly into a current account mortgage, this reduces the capital balance. Because the interest is calculated daily on this reduced balance, you will save a lot in interest charges. The trick, though, is leaving your income in the mortgage for as long as possible. Unfortunately, for most people, bills and living expenses must be paid each month and funds have to be drawn off the mortgage. As funds are drawn to pay for these bills the mortgage balance will increase, and as a result so will the interest charges. Using a credit card to pay for the majority of your monthly expenses will in effect defer the expenditure. This enables you to leave your income in the mortgage longer and continue to receive lower interest charges.

There will be times when you need cash, and this can be drawn off the mortgage by using the mortgage debit card. Never use a credit card to withdraw cash, as cash withdrawals attract fees.

Managing the credit card
Using a credit card this way requires good management and discipline on behalf of the user. So long as the user pays the balance of the credit card when it is due, they will not pay any interest charges. A good credit card can offer up to 56–57 days interest-free credit. Some credit card providers charge a yearly fee – the amount of these charges will vary depending on the credit card provider and the type of credit card you are using. However, if you use the credit card properly, this yearly fee will be negligible compared to the convenience and savings that can be achieved.

Obtaining benefits and perks
Many credit card providers offer 'perks and benefits' for using their credit card. These benefits can include air miles, cash back point schemes, travel accident insurance cover, travel discounts and so on. Obviously the more you use the card the more benefits will be accrued. If you use the card to pay for your groceries, fuel, utilities and so on, it won't take long to build up some very valuable savings and benefits.

CASE STUDIES

Natalie makes her decision
Natalie has chosen to refinance her interest-only mortgage to a current account mortgage. She has decided on the capital repayment method. Having her income paid directly into the mortgage will reduce the amount of accounts she presently uses. The flexibility suits her situation well, as her income can be erratic at times. Leaving her savings in the mortgage will also reduce the amount of interest she has to pay. Being a highly disciplined person

she will use a credit card to defer her monthly expenses, saving even more interest charges.

John chooses flexibility

John feels a flexible capital repayment mortgage will provide him with the flexibility he is after. Being conservative by nature, he feels the current account mortgage is a bit too technical for him. The flexible mortgage will allow him to make lump sum payments and pay his repayments fortnightly. Leaving any savings he has in the mortgage will also reduce the amount of interest he will repay. John will try to find a lender who offers a capped rate. If need be, he will accept a fixed rate.

Ross chooses the flexible mortgage

Ross feels the flexible capital repayment mortgage will adapt to his changing circumstances. It will allow him to take a payment holiday when the baby is born. Ross will look for a lender who calculates interest daily and charges it monthly or quarterly in arrears, enabling him to make fortnightly payments.

QUESTIONS AND ANSWERS

Do all lenders who provide flexible mortgages calculate interest daily and charge the interest monthly or quarterly in arrears?

The majority of lenders do, although the term 'flexible' can be used quite liberally. A good flexible mortgage will have the interest calculated and charged this way. In addition to this it should have all the features outlined in this chapter. No redemption penalties or limitations should apply.

Are my savings at risk by putting them in my mortgage?

No, your savings have actually been used to pay down the mortgage balance. No matter what happens, the lender cannot increase the amount you owe.

I'm not disciplined to use a credit card to defer expenditure. Is it essential to use a credit card with a current account mortgage?

No, you will still benefit greatly by having your earnings paid into a current account mortgage. Although a credit card when used properly can save you money, it can also cost you money if you do not use it properly or are undisciplined. If you are comfortable using a credit card this way use it, if not don't use it.

PERSONAL MORTGAGE AUDIT

- Does your present mortgage provide you with the flexibility you need?

- Would a flexible or current account mortgage suit your present and future needs?

- Do you have the discipline required to operate a current account mortgage properly?

- Do you consistently save each month? Could these savings be put to better use by leaving them in your mortgage?

7
Choosing the Right Lender

> A bank is a place that will lend you money if you can prove you don't need it.
>
> *Bob Hope*

With over 200 mortgage providers in the United Kingdom at present, there is certainly no shortage of choice for the borrower. Although a large building society or high street bank may seem to be the most logical and convenient choice, they may not always be the cheapest, or the most flexible. Recent years have seen an increasing number of lenders enter the mortgage market. Small and dynamic specialist lenders are consistently taking a larger slice of the mortgage services pie. Large supermarket chains such as Sainsburys have also entered the financial services market.

All this competition provides the borrower with a level of choice never seen before, resulting in better services and products for the borrower in the long run. Unfortunately an increase in choice can sometimes lead to confusion. This chapter will endeavour to remove any confusion you may have, providing information about the various lenders available. It will also explain the advantages and disadvantages of each, helping you to choose the right lender.

UNCOVERING THE MORTGAGE CODE

When choosing a mortgage lender, ensure they subscribe to the mortgage code. The Code of Mortgage Lending Practice took effect on 1 July 1997. This is a voluntary code, and those lenders that subscribe to it undertake to conform to its 10 key commitments, covering good lending practice, conduct of business and services provided to the customer.

To ensure compliance with the code, lenders that subscribe to it are monitored by an independent review body for the Banking and Mortgage Codes. The lender must also be a member of one of the following recognised complaints schemes:

- the Banking Ombudsman Scheme
- the Building Societies Ombudsman Scheme
- the Mortgage Code Arbitration Scheme.

Offering levels of service
Under the code, the lenders that subscribe to it are obliged at the outset to confirm, in writing, which one of the following three levels of service they will provide to the customer:

- advice and recommendation
- information on the different types of mortgage products available
- information on a single mortgage product only.

Advice and recommendation
The lender undertakes to provide to the borrower the most suitable mortgage in its range of products and to explain in writing the reasons for this. This means that if an endowment or PEP mortgage is not a suitable mortgage for you, the lender will not force you into one.

Information on the different types of mortgage products
The lender will provide information on various mortgage products offered by them, so the borrower may then make an informed decision on which mortgage best suits their needs.

Information on a single mortgage product only
The lender provides information on just one mortgage product, or information on a mortgage the borrower chose of their own volition.

Providing other information
Under the code the lender will also undertake to provide the borrower with the following information before finalising the mortgage:

- the type of interest rate, whether it is fixed, variable, capped, etc.
- the repayment method used and the repayment terms available
- disclosure of any redemption penalties applicable

Choosing the Right Lender

- whether the mortgage is portable
- disclosure of any fees and charges applicable to the mortgage
- whether compulsory insurances have to be taken out with the lender
- notification of what insurances are a condition of the mortgage and whose responsibility it is to ensure they are taken out
- details of any insurance products available through the lender
- what the repayments may be after a fixed term or a discounted period ends
- information about when the borrower's personal information can be handed to a credit reference agency
- information on 'MIRAS' mortgage interest relief
- whether a high lending fee is payable and an explanation of the terms and conditions
- information on failure to make suitable repayment arrangements
- assurance that adequate repayment methods are in place and notification of whose responsibility this is.

The above list is only a brief sample of the information a subscribing lender will supply. It is interesting to note that nothing is mentioned about the interest calculation and charging methods a lender may use. Other areas the mortgage code covers are:

- lending
- terms and conditions
- charges
- confidentiality
- financial difficulties
- complaints.

Choosing a lender that subscribes to the code will ensure you receive the very best service, advice and impartial information. For more comprehensive information about the Mortgage Code and to obtain a full list of the subscribing lenders, contact the Council of Mortgage Lenders whose address is given at the back of this book.

ANALYSING THE VARIOUS MORTGAGE LENDERS

Building societies have in the past provided more than 60 per cent of mortgages in the United Kingdom. The high street banks provide just under 30 per cent, and the remainder are provided by an assortment of other lenders such as specialist lenders, insurance companies, foreign banks, etc. As a rule-of-thumb, the larger the financial institution the greater the chance that they will be less flexible and have more rigid lending guidelines. A lender that has a large number of branches is also likely to have higher overhead costs than a smaller institution. In order to recover higher overhead costs, the larger banks and building societies may charge higher interest rates and/or impose higher fees, charges and penalties than the smaller lenders.

Using building societies

Traditionally building societies have been the first port of call for many people when seeking a mortgage. Building societies have been providing mortgage products for over one hundred years and mortgage products represent a large percentage of their business. Building societies vary considerably in size and many can be found on most high streets making them extremely convenient. Biggest is not always best and it is usually the smaller building societies that provide the best deals and customer service. Building societies have in the past tended to be more compassionate towards borrowers who have difficulties meeting repayments.

Regardless of whether they are convenient or compassionate to their borrowers, many building societies calculate and charge interest in advance. Before you proceed any further, your first question to any building society you are presently dealing with or are considering using is whether they calculate and charge interest in advance.

Advantages
- Conveniently located on most high streets.
- Many years of lending experience.
- Tend to be more compassionate to borrowers with financial difficulties.
- They are easily approachable with designated lending officers.

Disadvantages
- May impose restrictions on lump sum payments and the frequency with which payments can be made.
- Redemption penalties usually apply to mortgage products.
- The interest calculation and charging methods may not benefit the borrower.

Using banks
English banks have traditionally been old-fashioned and resistant to change. They may seem to be a logical place to visit when shopping for a mortgage. However, they can be very rigid in their lending practices and may be unwilling to negotiate on the rates and terms. The large high street banks generally offer traditional mortgage products only and may impose payment restrictions and penalties. Nevertheless, there are a handful of leading banks that do provide very flexible mortgage products. Like building societies, banks may also calculate and charge interest yearly in advance. You should always ask the particular bank you are presently using, or considering using, how they calculate and charge the interest and what payment restrictions and penalties they impose.

Advantages
- Convenient – many banks have large branch networks.
- Easily approachable with designated lending officers.
- Offer a large range of services other than mortgage products.

Disadvantages
- May not negotiate on fees and charges.
- The mortgage products they offer may not be flexible.
- May impose restrictions on lump sum payment amounts and the frequency with which payments can be made.
- The interest calculation and charging methods may not benefit the borrower.
- Rigid lending practices may make it hard to get the mortgage.

Using insurance companies
A number of insurance companies now offer their own range of mortgage products. Legal and General, for instance, offers the

'Flexible Reserve' mortgage. Insurance companies may also offer other bank and building society mortgage products through their network of advisers and also directly over the telephone. Insurance companies do not have large branch networks like the banks and building societies and this may make them less convenient to deal with. The insurance companies that develop and provide their own mortgage products do, however, offer the borrower other facilities, such as:

- access to 24-hour telephone banking
- computer banking (in some cases)
- providing cheque books
- providing debit card Automated Teller Machine (ATM) access
- provision for direct debit and standing orders.

Advantages
- Interest rates may be lower because of lower overheads.
- Flexible lending criteria.
- Insurances and investments offered.
- Insurance company mortgage products offered may be flexible.

Disadvantages
- No branch networks.
- Lack of banking facilities and other banking services.
- The borrower may be required to take the insurance company's insurance products and investments.

Using specialist lenders

These are also known as **centralised lenders** as they do not have branch networks like banks and building societies. They generally operate from one location, and as a result, generally have lower overhead costs. Specialist lenders, as the name suggests, specialise in mortgages and the related products only. Lower overhead costs enable them to offer slightly lower interest rates than the larger banks and building societies. They are usually small enough to move quickly to respond to market needs and are dynamic in their approach to developing new products and customer services.

Specialist lenders have in the past relied on networks of advisers and introducers to sell their range of mortgage products. Many specialist lenders can now be contacted directly via the telephone. Specialist lenders such as Mortgage Trust and Virgin Direct have developed some extremely flexible mortgage products. Mortgage Trust offers the 'Current Account Mortgage' and Virgin Direct provides 'The One Account'. Although specialist lenders do not have the branch networks like large banks and building societies, they do provide a wide range of facilities for the borrower, such as:

- debit card Automated Teller Machine (ATM) access
- access to 24-hour telephone banking
- cheque books and switch cards
- provision for direct debits and standing orders.

Advantages
- With lower overheads they can generally offer lower interest rates.
- The majority calculate the interest daily and charge monthly or quarterly in arrears.
- They offer a large range of highly flexible mortgage products.
- Being mortgage specialists they usually have flexible lending guidelines.
- They generally do not impose restrictions on payment amounts or repayment frequency.
- Little or no redemption penalties are charged.

Disadvantages
- Lack of branch networks may make them less convenient.
- They do not offer the wide range of other services banks and building societies provide.

CONSIDERING OTHER MORTGAGE PROVIDERS

Obtaining a mortgage is not just limited to banks and building societies these days. You may be surprised to discover some of the many companies involved in the financial services market.

Using supermarkets
Some large supermarket chains, such as Sainsbury's and Tesco's,

have entered the financial services market, providing personal loans and mortgage products. It's a smart move as these retail giants endeavour to cash in on their massive customer base. The range of mortgage products they provide is generally limited, although over time this may improve.

Finance and credit companies
Some finance houses and credit companies provide mortgages. These mortgage products are generally interest-only mortgages, at relatively high interest rates, with high redemption penalties. Their lending guidelines tend to be more flexible and they may lend larger amounts than other lenders. It must be noted that they are usually less tolerant of borrowers who find themselves in financial difficulties.

Local authorities
Tenants living in council houses who decide to exercise their 'right to buy' option may apply to the local authority for a mortgage. A mortgage may also be granted by some authorities to people wanting to buy and renovate derelict houses.

Builder arranged
Organising your mortgage through a builder may seem convenient, but it could come at a great cost. Builders do not actually finance the mortgage themselves, they merely arrange the mortgage through a lending institution. A builder may also receive commissions from the mortgage they arrange. There may be many clauses in the mortgage document that could leave the borrower vulnerable to increased interest charges and also provide loopholes for the builder. Be wary of offers of 100 per cent mortgages and lower than normal interest rates, as these inducements to buy could end up costing you more.

UTILISING MORTGAGE ADVISERS

A mortgage adviser or finance intermediary who subscribes to the Mortgage Code can help you find the best lender with the best mortgage. So long as they are not tied to one company, or offer products from only one source, they can provide you with good independent advice and impartial information. Generally mortgage brokers and independent financial advisers (IFA's) have up-to-date information on a large number of lenders and mortgage products.

Many will even visit you in the comfort and safety of your home. This can save you a lot of time as compared with you visiting the lenders. Advisers generally receive their remuneration from the lender directly and **should not charge you any additional fees**.

Advisers and the Mortgage Code
Before 30 April 1998, mortgage advisers and finance intermediaries were not included in the Mortgage Code. Those advisers who now voluntarily subscribe to the code must disclose to the borrower certain information about the level of service and advice they will provide, such as:

- whom they work for, whether they are independent or a tied agent
- what commissions they will receive
- what service and advice they will provide.

To qualify under the code they must be a member of the Mortgage Code Arbitration Scheme for handling complaints. They are also monitored for compliance to the code by the Independent Review Body for the Banking and Mortgage Codes. You should always endeavour to use an adviser or lender that subscribes to the Mortgage Code. For a full list of subscribing finance advisers and intermediaries, contact the Mortgage Code Register of Intermediaries, whose address is located at the back of this book under Useful Addresses.

Using mortgage brokers
These professionals specialise purely in mortgage products and the associated insurances. However, they cannot sell investments such as personal equity plans or endowment policies. Mortgage brokers generally have access to a large number of lenders and a wide variety of mortgage products. They provide advice on which mortgage would best suit your needs and they also act as a middleman between you and the lender. Make sure the broker isn't a tied agent or insurance representative.

Using independent financial advisers (IFAs)
IFAs can provide advice on a wide range of mortgage products and investments. They must provide their customers with the best advice for their particular needs and circumstances. IFAs are totally independent of any lender or insurance company. They generally

have up-to-date information on a large number of lenders and mortgage products.

Using insurance representatives and tied agents

This group of advisers are generally employed by just one company. They can usually only sell you mortgage and insurance products that their particular company offers. They may also advise you to purchase their products even though you may be able to source more competitive products elsewhere. A good number of mortgage advisers within estate agencies are tied agents. Many estate agencies are in fact owned by banks and building societies, so you can imagine whose mortgage products they will be trying to sell.

CASE STUDIES

Natalie looks for independent advice

Natalie's busy work schedule means that she does not have time to look for a suitable lender that offers a current account mortgage. So she has decided to use an independent mortgage broker who subscribes to the Mortgage Code. She has asked the Mortgage Code Register of Intermediaries to send her a full list of mortgage brokers. She will contact a number of mortgage brokers to determine whether they charge any fees for their service, what service and advice they provide and whether they are independent. She is interested in finding out more about the specialist lenders, so she will ask the broker when she has chosen one.

John finds it hard to change

In the past John has always used his bank for all his financial needs. Although he is not happy with his present mortgage, he will check with his present lender to see what they can offer. He is prepared to look elsewhere and move his business to another bank if they can offer him a better deal. He will only consider a bank if they subscribe to the Mortgage Code. John does not feel comfortable using an adviser or any other type of lender.

Ross is confused

Being a first-time buyer, Ross is bewildered by the choice of lenders available. He has decided to use an independent financial adviser who subscribes to the Mortgage Code to help him find the right lender. He has asked the Mortgage Code Register of Intermediaries to send him a full list of all subscribing IFAs.

QUESTIONS AND ANSWERS

I have only ever used a building society for my mortgage needs. Are specialist lenders safe to use?

Yes. Because you are borrowing money from them and not investing money, you basically have nothing to lose and everything to gain.

How can I tell whether a mortgage adviser is independent or a tied agent?

Basically you just have to ask them. Any mortgage intermediary who subscribes to the Mortgage Code must tell you whether they are a tied agent or an independent. Companies that sell endowment or pension mortgages under the Financial Services Act must also disclose to the customer whether they are an independent providing unbiased advice, or a tied agent selling one company's products.

PERSONAL MORTGAGE AUDIT

- Are there any reasons why you would not consider using an independent mortgage adviser or intermediary who subscribes to the Mortgage Code?

- Would you consider a mortgage lender that does not provide normal banking services? If not, what are your reasons for this?

- What major factors would influence you in deciding which lender you would use?

8
Establishing a Mortgage

> Take care to get what you like or you will be forced to like what you get.
>
> *George Bernard Shaw*

Much time is often spent finding the perfect house, yet very little time and thought is usually given to finding the right mortgage and lender. Spending more time to find the right mortgage and lender before you start looking for a property can save you from a lot of expensive mistakes. This chapter will help you to:

- understand all the associated costs of buying and selling a property
- refinance your mortgage and deal with negative equity
- calculate how much you can borrow and afford to borrow
- apply for a mortgage and increase your chances of approval
- deal with a rejected application and provide alternative avenues
- generally avoid unexpected charges and expensive mistakes.

PURCHASING YOUR FIRST HOME

Asking for assistance
Buying your first home could be either your greatest experience, or one you wish never happened. Avoiding the latter will be dependent upon the amount of homework you do before you start looking. You can glean a lot of information and help from parents, friends and relatives who have already bought a property. Asking advice from these people may also help you to avoid any expensive mistakes they may have experienced.

Establishing a savings history
Lenders carefully examine applicants' bank statements, looking for proof of a consistent savings history. Usually the minimum period of time they will consider is six months and lenders do not usually accept deposits if they are a gift. A regular savings history demonstrates to the lender that you are disciplined and have the capacity to repay the mortgage. The better your savings history, the better your chances of obtaining a mortgage.

Saving for a deposit
Many first-home buyers find it difficult to save a large deposit, generally only scraping together the bare minimum required. This problem usually stems from their inability to sacrifice a little, for a short period of time. If you make a concerted and disciplined effort to reduce expenses and curb unnecessary spending, you will find you can save a large deposit in a relatively short period of time. Drafting up a budget can highlight areas that could be reduced or cut out altogether. The majority of mortgage lenders will lend up to 90–95 per cent of the property's value, requiring a minimum of 5–10 per cent deposit. The more deposit you put down, the lower the amount of money you have to borrow and also the amount of MIG premium you may be charged.

Pre-qualifying for a mortgage
Before looking for a house, it may pay you to get a lender to pre-qualify you for a mortgage. This will give you an idea of how much you can borrow, saving you from choosing a house that is out of your reach. It will also give you a fairly accurate idea of what fees and charges you will have to pay. In most cases you will not be obligated to take the lender's mortgage for which you pre-qualified. Never feel obliged to take the lender's mortgage, especially if their interest rates or charges increase.

ADDING UP THE COSTS OF BUYING AND SELLING A PROPERTY

Calculating the costs of buying a property
There are many fees and charges associated with buying a property, and we will cover the common fees you could expect to pay. Before you choose the house you want to buy, you should calculate all the expenses involved. This will ensure you will not over-commit yourself and place unnecessary strain on your finances.

Mortgage arrangement fees
These fees are also commonly referred to as an 'establishment fee'. The majority of lenders charge them to cover administration costs involved in setting up the mortgage. Many lenders do not charge any arrangement fees and some may be prepared to negotiate how much they will charge, so check with the lender.

Mortgage indemnity guarantee premium (MIG)
These premiums are usually charged if you borrow over a certain loan-to-value ratio, usually starting at 75–80 per cent. MIG premiums are explained in great detail in Chapter 2, Mortgage indemnity guarantee premiums.

Lender's valuation fee
Valuation report fees vary from lender to lender. Lenders use this report to determine the property's value, so they can determine how much they will lend against it. Valuation fees are usually calculated on the value of the property and the borrower will usually pay for this. Ask your lender how much this will cost.

Lender's solicitor's fee
There is presently no statutory scale of fees for the production of mortgage documents and all relevant legal work for the mortgage. As such these fees will also vary from lender to lender. You will have to pay these fees in addition to your own solicitor/conveyancer. Ask your lender how much they charge.

Stamp duty
This is a tax paid on the purchase price of a property that exceeds £60,000.00. The present rate of stamp duty charged is 1 per cent. For example, if you purchased a house worth £60,000.00 you would not pay any stamp duty. If you bought a house worth £65,000.00, you would pay £650.00 in stamp duty.

Conveyancing fee
Choose your solicitor or conveyancer with care as they have no restrictions on the amount they can charge. It is worthwhile contacting a number of solicitors and licensed conveyancers and comparing their prices. Once you have made your decision, ask for a written quotation. Some will charge a flat fee for the work carried out, while others may charge anything up to and beyond 1 per cent of the purchase price of the property plus VAT.

Establishing a Mortgage

Land registry fee
These fees are paid on all property purchases regardless of their value. The charges are based on a statutory scale of fees which can usually be obtained from your real estate agent, lender or the land registry.

Local authority searches
On your behalf the solicitor or conveyancer will request a search from the local authority, for information about any future plans that may affect the property. The search will provide information such as any planned roads to be constructed nearby, any railway lines being built, development of large commercial buildings and so on. The fee charged for this search is fixed and generally costs around £60.00. The minimum search fee throughout Greater London is £100.00.

Surveyor's fee
A structural survey on a property will uncover any major problems or defects with the house. Unless the house or flat is newly built, you should seriously consider a survey. There are three main types of survey reports that can be requested:

1. *The valuation report* – this report is completed regardless of whether a structural survey is done or not. The fees are usually calculated on the property's value – allow from £150 to £250. The valuation report uncovers major defects that may affect the property's value. It does not, however, uncover any other problems such as damp and general disrepair.

2. *An intermediate survey or home buyer's report* – this report usually uncovers major structural defects, including items such as woodworm, wood rot and damp. The surveyor will not usually inspect the roof or under the floor boards. The costs are usually calculated on the value of the property, so allow from £30 to £40 per £10,000.00 of property value.

3. *The building or full structural survey* – this is a comprehensive report which includes a full survey of the property. This report is recommended for older homes or properties that have add-ons or conversions. Allow from £300 to £1,000 plus VAT for this type of report.

Removal costs
Do it yourself or hire a professional? That is the question. It may

work out that the cost of moving yourself would be as expensive as hiring a professional remover. When you add up the costs of hiring a van or truck including VAT, packing boxes and petrol, and when your time is taken into consideration, it may be worth while letting someone else do it. Before you decide to do it yourself, you should ring around for at least five quotes from professional removal firms. If, however, you are a first-home buyer, you may only have a small amount of furniture which could be easily moved in a van.

Calculating the costs of selling a property
As with buying a property, there are many fees involved in selling one. If you are also buying a property you will have to allow for the costs of both.

Estate agent's fee
Allow up to 1.5–2 per cent of the purchase price of the property for the estate agent's commission.

Solicitor or conveyancer fee
The fees charged for this service, as discussed earlier, are not set and a solicitor or conveyancer can charge at their discretion. You should obtain a number of quotations before instructing a solicitor or conveyancer to act on your behalf. Allow up to 1 per cent of the property's value (plus VAT) for this fee.

Mortgage redemption penalty
This is discussed in great detail in Chapter 2, avoiding redemption penalties. A penalty may be charged for paying off a mortgage during a fixed, capped or discount interest rate period. Some mortgages, however, are portable, allowing the borrower to take the mortgage with them without incurring additional fees and charges. Check with your lender whether your mortgage is subject to any redemption penalties.

Use the table in Figure 10 to calculate your total costs of buying and selling a property.

REFINANCING YOUR PRESENT MORTGAGE

Refinancing a mortgage is also commonly referred to as remortgaging. There are a number of reasons why people choose to refinance their mortgage, such as:

CALCULATING THE COSTS OF BUYING AND SELLING A PROPERTY	
Buying	
Mortgage arrangement fee	£
Mortgage indemnity premium	£
Lender's valuation fee	£
Lender's solicitor's fee	£
Stamp duty	£
Conveyancing fee	£
Land registry free	£
Local authority searches fee	£
Surveyor's fee	£
Removal costs	£
TOTAL COST OF BUYING	£
Selling	
Estate agent's commission	£
Solicitor/conveyancer fees	£
Mortgage redemption penalty	£
TOTAL COST OF SELLING	£

Fig. 10. Calculating the costs of buying and selling a property.

- They are presently locked into a high fixed interest rate, when current interest rates are much lower.
- Their present mortgage has interest calculated and charged in advance, rather than calculated daily and charged monthly or quarterly in arrears.
- Their present mortgage has many restrictions and limitations, not allowing them to pay as much or as often as they would like.
- They are moving home and their mortgage is not portable.
- They have decided to consolidate a number of debts into one.

Refinancing your mortgage can provide you with real savings, so long as you don't refinance to a mortgage that is no better than the one you already have. This may seem like common sense, yet it can happen. Many people do not do their homework and fail to calculate whether refinancing will benefit them.

Deciding whether to refinance

People who have had a mortgage for a number of years should as a matter of course have a look around at what is on offer by other lenders. Your present lender may have been competitive when you first took out the mortgage, but may not be that competitive now. You should ask your lender the following questions prior to looking at what is on offer elsewhere:

- What is the present mortgage balance?
- How is the interest calculated and charged?
- What is the present interest rate?
- How much is my monthly mortgage repayment?
- What payment amount and payment restrictions apply?
- Are there any partial redemption penalties? If so, what are they?
- How much will it cost me to cash in my mortgage early?
- How long does the present discounted, fixed or capped rate period last for?

Negotiating with your present lender

It may be that the mortgage you presently have is a good mortgage, although the present interest rate is not so good. Very few people realise they can actually negotiate a better interest rate with their lender. By negotiating a reduced interest rate deal, you can avoid any additional costs associated with refinancing to another lender. If, however, they calculate and charge interest in advance, or they impose many payment restrictions and/or redemption penalties, then regardless of whether they can reduce the interest rate, you should seriously consider refinancing elsewhere. You should ask your present lender the following questions to see what type of deal they could offer you:

- Can you offer me a new discounted, fixed, capped or variable rate deal?
- What will the new interest rate be?

- What will my repayments be for the new deal?
- Is the interest calculated and charged the same way as my present mortgage?
- What additional fees will be charged for setting up the new deal?
- Are there any redemption penalties? If so, what are they?
- What restrictions will apply to payment frequency and payment amount for the new deal?

You can then use this information to compare against the various offers from other lenders you approach.

Weighing up the costs of refinancing

Before you make the decision to refinance your present mortgage, you should weigh up the total savings that could be achieved against the total cost of changing to another lender. You can determine this by using the simple calculations in Figure 11.

CALCULATING YOUR MONTHLY SAVINGS	
Present monthly repayment	£ .
Less new monthly repayment	£ .
TOTAL MONTHLY SAVINGS	£ .

CALCULATING THE TOTAL COST OF REFINANCING	
Any redemption fees payable, existing	£ .
Arrangement fee, new mortgage	£ .
Valuation fee, new mortgage	£ .
Solicitors/legal fees, new mortgage	£ .
Mortgage indemnity MIG, new mortgage	£ .
TOTAL COST OF REFINANCING	£ .

Fig. 11. Calculating the costs of refinancing.

Calculating your potential monthly savings
On paper the savings may initially appear minimal. However, if you are refinancing a mortgage that has the interest calculated and charged in advance to one that has interest calculated daily and charged monthly in arrears, you will find the savings that can be achieved by using various reduction methods will result in larger savings.

Calculating the total cost of refinancing
At all times throughout the refinancing process your main objective is to save money. If the savings that could be achieved outweigh the costs involved in refinancing your present mortgage, you should approach your existing lender again to see whether they could counter-offer the new deal. If it is at all possible to stay with your current lender, you should give them every chance to match the other deals on offer. This will save you the costs associated with refinancing.

DEALING WITH NEGATIVE EQUITY

A negative equity situation occurs when the total value of loans secured against a property exceeds the property's value. Prior to the last recession lenders eagerly handed out mortgages of up to 100 per cent of the property's value. Basically you could borrow £80,000.00 on a property valued at £80,000.00. However, after the recession hit and the dust had settled, it was evident that 100 per cent mortgages were a very costly mistake for both the lender and the borrower. Many lenders learnt some very valuable lessons and as a result, 100 per cent mortgages are now harder to come by.

Examining negative equity schemes
Although housing prices have risen since the market slumped, you may still find you are in a negative equity situation. As the need grew to help those unfortunate people who found themselves in this predicament, the lenders created special negative equity mortgage schemes. There are primarily three types of negative equity scheme on offer by a handful of lenders today:

1. A scheme whereby the negative equity from an existing property can be transferred to a new property.
2. A scheme which allows you to borrow more than the price of

the new property to cover the negative equity difference.

3. A scheme which allows you to purchase a new property and leave the existing property to be rented out, until such time as it can be sold to cover the negative equity.

Not all lenders offer these types of negative equity schemes. The ones that do may lend up to 125 per cent of the property's value. A borrower will generally pay a slightly higher repayment to help pay down the negative equity portion. Arrangement fees and MIG premiums will usually apply, making negative equity schemes quite costly. Unfortunately many people do need these schemes, as they may have to relocate because of a job transfer, or a larger house is required as their family grows and so on. Lenders offering these schemes include Barclays Bank, Bank of Scotland Centrebank and Cheltenham & Gloucester.

Reducing your negative equity
Making overpayments to your mortgage to reduce the negative equity is a less expensive way of dealing with this problem. Although your repayments may be higher, you will not pay the large expenses associated with negative equity schemes. If the mortgage you have restricts you from making overpayments, or redemption penalties are charged, speak to your lender to see what arrangements can be made. If nothing can be arranged, you could invest the extra funds into a savings account, until you have sufficient funds to clear the negative equity and move house.

CHOOSING THE MORTGAGE AND LENDER YOU WANT TO USE

Deciding which mortgage you want
Before you decide which lender you want to use, you should choose which type of mortgage product you want. There is very little point deciding on a particular lender, if they cannot supply you with the type of mortgage you are looking for. The mortgage you choose should not only cater for your present situation, but also provide for your future needs.

Selecting the lender
When you have decided which type of mortgage you want, it is time to find the lender offering the best deal. A mortgage adviser can be useful in supplying you with a list of various lenders that offer the

type of mortgage you require, providing they are independent and not a tied agent.

Checking the lender's fees and charges
An important area to check with potential lenders is their initial establishment costs and related charges. Ask the lender for a tariff sheet which lists the fees and charges for the services they provide. Listed below are some questions you could ask them:

- Are there any mortgage arrangement fees? If so, how much are they?
- Do you charge any valuation and or solicitor fees? If so, how much will they be?
- Are there any insurance products that must be purchased as a condition of the mortgage? (If so, this will reduce your rights to shop around and obtain the most competitive insurance products.)
- Do you charge 'MIG' (mortgage indemnity premium)? If so, how much will it be?
- How do you calculate and charge the interest? (Only accept daily reducible interest calculation and monthly or quarterly in arrears charging methods.)

Once you have determined which lenders you wish to use, you should select the one offering the best mortgage deal. The more homework you do before you make a decision, the better your decision will be. A little time spent shopping around could save you a lot of money.

CALCULATING HOW MUCH YOU CAN BORROW

Defining income
When a lender uses the term 'income', they are usually referring to gross basic salary, before tax or any other deductions. They will usually only take into consideration any **guaranteed** overtime, commission and bonuses. The lender will generally request written confirmation from your employer, that these guaranteed incomes will continue to be paid in the future. You can use the guide in Figure 12 to help you calculate your yearly gross income.

Establishing a Mortgage

CALCULATING YOUR GROSS INCOME		
	Borrower 1	Borrower 2
Gross yearly basic salary	£	£
Guaranteed yearly overtime	£	£
Guaranteed yearly bonuses	£	£
Guaranteed yearly commission	£	£
Total gross yearly income	£	£

Fig. 12. Calculating your gross income.

Utilising the income multiplier

The majority of lenders use factors which are multiplied by the borrower's yearly income to calculate the maximum amount they are prepared to lend. A lender will usually allow a single person to borrow up to 2.5 to 3 times their gross yearly income. For a couple who are both earning an income, a lender will usually allow up to 2.5 or 3 times the higher income, plus 1 to 1.5 times the lower income. For example, if one partner earns £25,000.00 and the other earns £12,000.00, the calculation might look like this:

Partner 1: £25,000.00 × 3 = £75,000.00
Partner 2: £12,000.00 × 1 = £12,000.00

Maximum amount that can be borrowed = £87,000.00

Not all lenders use the same multiple factors and these can also be affected by the current rates of interest. Generally the higher the interest rates the lower the multiples, and the lower the interest rates the higher the multiples. At times a lender may lend beyond the multiple factors, but this is usually only if the borrower is an existing customer with a good savings history. To calculate the maximum amount you could borrow, use the income multiplier in Figure 13.

INCOME MULTIPLIER		
Total gross yearly income, borrower 1	£	
X gross income by lender's multiplier factor		£
Total gross yearly income, borrower 2	£	
X gross income by lender's multiplier factor		£
Add the two factored amounts together to determine how much you can borrow		£

Fig. 13. Income multiplier.

Self-employed applicants

Most lenders will require self-employed applicants to provide no less than the last three years audited accounts. They generally take the average of the income earned over these three years. Some lenders may base it on the prior year's profits, but they will check the previous years' figures to ensure you didn't just have a one-off boom year.

Calculating how much you can afford to pay

The income factors lenders use ensure the borrower has the financial capacity to make the mortgage repayments. These factors are generally based on an average person's income and expenses. Unfortunately not everyone has average income and expenses. A person who travels long distances to work will have higher travelling expenses than someone who lives close to their work. Other things such as the prospect of having children will also affect a person's financial situation. Only you will truly know how much you can afford to pay each month and what future plans will affect your ability to meet the mortgage repayments.

Utilising an expenses checklist

Drafting an expenses checklist will provide you with a precise figure of how much you can afford to repay each month. The checklist provided in Figure 14 is a guide which includes the usual expenses you could expect to pay. This checklist should be used as a guide only and adapted to your own personal situation. Include any other expenses you may have, incorporating any possible future changes to your financial position.

This checklist can also be used as your monthly budget once you have established the mortgage. Your success will depend on your ability to manage your finances properly. The checklist provided has been divided into three main areas, helping you to highlight areas that could be reduced.

Necessary adjustable expenses
This refers to expenses that are essential for daily living. They are adjustable because these items, such as telephone bills, electricity and fuel costs, can all be reduced with a little care.

Necessary fixed expenses
These expenses are items essential to daily living which are reasonably hard to alter. In saying this, insurance premiums can be in some cases reduced by shopping around.

EXPENSES CHECKLIST

Necessary adjustable expenses   £
Telephone   ....
Petrol   ....
Fares   ....
Gas   ....
Electricity   ....
Chemist   ....
School books/Uniforms   ....
Life insurance   ....
Repairs to home   ....
Groceries/food   ....
Credit card payments   ....
Loan payments   ....
   Subtotal necessary adjustable expenses   _____

Necessary fixed expenses   £
Council tax   ....
Water rates   ....
Home contents insurance   ....
Home building insurance   ....
Insurance vehicle 1   ....
Insurance vehicle 2   ....
Servicing and repairs   ....
Road tax and MOT   ....
Television licence   ....
School fees   ....
Dentist   ....
Medical   ....
Pensions   ....
   Subtotal necessary fixed expenses   _____

Discretionary expenses   £
Car breakdown insurance   ....
Entertainment   ....
Cigarettes   ....
Clothes   ....
Newspaper   ....
Gifts   ....
Sports/hobbies   ....
Pets   ....
Baby sitting   ....
Subscriptions   ....
Holidays   ....
   Subtotal discretionary expenses   _____
(Add all subtotal expenses to arrive at the total
monthly expenses)   _____

Fig. 14. An expenses checklist.

Discretionary expenses
These expenses are items not generally considered essential for daily living. They are, in short, the 'wants' and not the 'needs'. It is usually these expenses that bite into a person's ability to save money, as many people tend to overspend in this area. Careful monitoring of these expenses can result in dramatic savings.

SUBMITTING A MORTGAGE APPLICATION

The mortgage application to settlement process can be quite an endurance test. Some lenders can take up to 4–6 weeks just to send out a written offer known as a mortgage certificate. The settlement process can then take anything up to 2–3 months to finalise. There are many things that you can do to expedite the application process and also improve your chances of approval.

Save time, and organise your documents.

Information required by a lender
The application stage can take some time to complete, usually because an applicant does not have the necessary documentation required close at hand. Listed below are the items a lender will generally ask for. If you are making a joint application you will need to provide these items for both of you.

- National Insurance number and tax reference
- minimum of last six months bank statements

- contract of employment, last three months payslips and P60
- your existing mortgage statements if you have one
- details of any loan agreements you may have outstanding
- proof of current address, e.g. council tax bill, utility bill
- a reference from your landlord if you are presently renting
- driver's licence and passport if available
- any life insurance policies
- the name, address and phone number of your employer
- last two to three years accounts or tax assessments if you are self-employed.

Completing the mortgage application

A mortgage application form can be quite involved. The information listed above will be needed to complete it. If you are not comfortable filling in the application yourself, ask your lender to do it for you. Make sure you dot the i's and cross the t's. Failure to fully complete the application is often one of the main reasons an approval is held up. If you are unsure about any questions on the application form, ask the lender.

Lending money for a purpose
Lenders tend to be wary if you are refinancing to consolidate debts. They may ask you questions to determine why you are consolidating debts, as you may be in financial difficulties. Don't be put off by their questions as they are only looking after their interests. So long as you are borrowing money for a reasonable purpose, a lender will not normally subject you to a barrage of questions.

Receiving mortgage approval

A lender will advise you verbally over the telephone that the application has been successful. They will then usually send you a mortgage certificate, providing written confirmation of the approval, usually subject to a valuation and a structural survey. The mortgage certificate will usually be valid for from 6 weeks to 3 months. Once the valuation, structural survey and any additional inspections have been completed, the lender will then notify you whether they will lend on the property, how much they will lend and the terms and conditions that apply.

Observing the mortgage conditions

Most lenders will provide you with a list of conditions which you have to meet. These can include:

- putting any disrepair right within a certain time frame
- not renting out the property without the permission of the lender
- keeping the property in good condition
- ensuring the property is insured at all times
- notifying the lender before applying for any additional mortgages
- notifying the lender of any local authority plans which could affect the property
- gaining permission from the lender before applying for any improvement grants, including carrying out any modifications to the property – this can include extensions, conversions and so on.

HANDLING A REJECTED APPLICATION

There are primarily four reasons why a mortgage application can be rejected:

- lack of capacity to repay the mortgage
- not meeting the lender's credit-score requirements
- adverse credit history
- unsuitable property.

You should ask the lender to tell you the reasons why your application was rejected. Usually it will be for one or a combination of the reasons listed above. If the application was rejected because of adverse credit, they may not disclose to you the exact nature of the adverse credit.

Lack of capacity

If you do not have sufficient income to borrow a specific amount of money, the lender will decline the application because of a lack of capacity. If this is the only reason for the rejection, you should ask the lender how much they would be prepared to lend. If, on the other hand, you are self-employed and your accounts do not show sufficient income, or you have only been in business for a short period of time, you may have a hard time finding a lender that can help you. There are many non-standard mortgage companies around which may be able to help. Some non-standard mortgage companies include Preferred Mortgages and The Money Shop.

Credit-scoring
A large percentage of lenders credit-score applicants to determine whether they fall into their risk category. Credit-scoring is a points system whereby certain aspects of the applicant's personal details are judged and assigned a certain amount of points. If the combined points do not satisfy the lender's minimum points requirement, the application will be declined. Areas in which an applicant may be credit-scored include the length of time in their employment, their age, the number of years they have been with their bank, how long have they lived at their address and so on. Every lender's credit-scoring system differs, so where you may not credit-score with one lender, you may credit-score with another.

Adverse credit
All lenders access an applicant's credit reference to determine whether they are a good credit risk or a bad credit risk. Adverse credit can include:

- slow payment history
- failure to pay bills such as utilities
- any court judgements lodged against you.

Credit reference agencies
Credit reference agencies are licensed under the Consumer Credit Act 1974. These particular organisations, under an agreement with financial institutions, can access information from computer systems across the country about an individual's creditworthiness. Information held by credit reference agencies can include:

- any bank accounts you have opened
- whether you have been made bankrupt
- any loans you have taken out, current and paid in full
- any credit cards you have
- any county court judgements listed against you

- any mortgage you may have
- failure to pay any bills, such as council tax
- whether you have provided fraudulent information.

The information they hold is usually accurate, although human error may result in incorrect information being held. If you find this is the case, you have to apply for a copy of your credit report and request that the report be amended. There are two main credit reference agencies in the United Kingdom: Experian Ltd and Equifax Europe (UK) Ltd – addresses are listed at the back of this book under Useful Addresses. To obtain a copy of your credit report from a credit reference agency, you need to write to them requesting it. They will usually charge a small fee such as £1–2 which you have to send with the letter. Make sure you send a cheque and not currency. The information they require from you is included in the letter template provided Figure 15.

Seeking alternative lenders
If you have adverse credit listed on your credit file, you may find it difficult to get a mortgage, depending on the severity and amount of the adverse credit listed. There are companies that specialise in providing mortgages to people who would not normally qualify. Some lenders who may be able to help are Preferred Mortgages and The Money Shop.

Unsuitable property
If this is the only reason for a declined application, then all you have to do is find a suitable property that the lender will accept.

CASE STUDIES

Natalie refinances with no fuss
Natalie received her list of intermediaries from the Mortgage Code Register of Intermediaries. She phoned five mortgage brokers and chose one that did not charge any fees for their service. The mortgage broker provided Natalie with two lenders that offered the current account mortgage loans. Natalie calculated the various charges and flexible features of both and made her decision. With the help of the mortgage broker she negotiated with the lender to waive the arrangement fees and solicitor costs. The mortgage broker helped her with the application and settlement process, ensuring a

[Insert your address]

[Insert particular credit agency's address]
Consumer Affairs Department

[Date]

RE: CONSUMER CREDIT ACT 1974

I wish to apply under section 158(1) of the above Act for a copy of the file (if any exists) held by you which relates to myself.

Please find my personal details including my current and previous addresses at which I have resided over the past 6 years. Should you have any information relating to me, please send me written details, along with explanatory notes of the Consumer's rights under Section 159 of the Consumer Credit Act 1974, to the above address.

Personal Details

Title: [i.e. Mr/Mrs] Christian Name(s):   Surname:

Present address details From: To:	Previous address details From: To:
Address:	Address:
Postal town:	Postal town:
County: Post code:	County: Post code:
Previous address details From: To:	Previous address details From: To:
Address:	Address:
Postal town:	Postal town:
County: Post code:	County: Post code:

I also enclose a cheque for the statutory fee of £____.____ to cover your expenses.
        [Only required if the particular credit agency requires it.]

Yours sincerely

[Signature]
[Your name]

Fig. 15. Obtaining your credit reference, letter template.

smooth transition from one mortgage to the other.

John goes it alone
John approached his bank first, but they did not have a flexible mortgage product to offer him. He then phoned a number of banks and was surprised that many larger banks did not offer them either. After much phoning around, John finally found two smaller banks that had them. After calculating and comparing the fees and charges, flexible features and the interest calculation and charging methods, John carefully made his decision. Although the bank he chose had a slightly higher interest rate, they could offer all the other banking services he wanted. John submitted an application and he was surprised at the speed with which the approval came through. The lender told John he had excellent stability in his job and residence, with an excellent credit history. The mortgage was settled two months later – slightly longer than he was initially told, but he was happy none the less.

Ross fails to do his homework
Ross and Cinzla found their dream home first, before contacting an independent financial adviser. The financial adviser supplied them with five different lenders that offered good flexible mortgage loans. Although the products each lender offered were very similar, he chose one particular lender because they did not charge any arrangement fees. With the help of the adviser he submitted the application. A few days later the lender called and told him the application was rejected because of adverse credit. Ross wrote to the credit reference agency requesting a copy of his credit file. When the credit file arrived, it showed an unpaid utility bill from his previous residence. After contacting the particular company, he paid the amount outstanding and received proof that it was satisfied. He contacted the lender and told them it was a genuine error and he had overlooked the bill when he moved from this address. After supplying the lender with proof that the debt was paid, they finally accepted the application. Unfortunately, because of the time taken to get the mortgage approved, the time limit elapsed on the house and the property was consequently sold to someone else. Now that they were pre-qualified for a mortgage, they eventually found another property and with the help of the adviser it went smoothly to settlement.

QUESTIONS AND ANSWERS

When should I start shopping around for a mortgage?

Before you buy the house! Many people make the mistake of finding a property first and then rushing into a mortgage to meet the purchase closing deadline. Before you buy a house, take your time to find the right mortgage and lender you want to use. Pre-qualify for the mortgage and then take your time to find the perfect house.

Why don't lenders accept deposits if they are gifts?

A mortgage is a large commitment to repay each month. The lender will therefore want to ensure you have both the commitment and the discipline to repay it. Saving a deposit shows the lender that you have the strength of character to take on this responsibility. If you are given something without earning it, this does not show the strength of character a lender is looking for. A lender will also check your bank statements for proof that the deposit was saved.

PERSONAL MORTGAGE AUDIT

- Is your present mortgage costing you more than it should? Are you aware of the mortgage deals on offer through other lenders? When was the last time you checked?

- If your property is in negative equity, rather than use a negative equity mortgage scheme, how long would it take you either to repay the negative equity portion or to save enough to pay it off?

- What expenses could be reduced to help you save more money towards a deposit?

9
Managing Your Mortgage

Creditors have better memories than debtors.
James Howell – Proverbs

Many people do not bother to check their mortgage statement because they find it too difficult to understand. These very people could be paying more fees and charges than they should, but are none the wiser. If you believed you were charged more than you should be charged, would you know how and where to complain? Or if you found yourself in financial difficulties, would you know where you could get help? This chapter will endeavour to help you understand a mortgage statement, how to make a complaint and how to obtain help with financial difficulties.

CHECKING YOUR MORTGAGE STATEMENT

It is very important to check your mortgage statement carefully. It is usually quite simple to spot a fee or charge on the statement, but without a tariffs sheet you may have little or no chance of understanding what it is for. Some lenders use elaborate jargon to camouflage the name for fees and charges.

Obtaining a tariff
A tariff will list all the fees and charges a lender may charge for any services rendered. The lender is also required under the Mortgage Code to set out the terms and conditions in plain language. However, judging by some of the jargon used by a few lenders, this hasn't caught on that well. Lenders who subscribe to the Mortgage Code must provide new borrowers and existing borrowers with a tariff. Under the Mortgage Code a lender is required to send the borrower a new tariff once a year, should any changes be made to their fees and charges. Arrears charges are usually the cause of many customer complaints. Many lenders fail to disclose the

potential charges clearly and concisely. If you feel you have been unduly over-charged, or you have been wrongly charged, you can make a complaint to the lender.

MAKING A COMPLAINT

Approaching your lender

If you have a complaint against a lender, you should contact them first and explain the problem. Make sure you write down the name of the person you speak to and the time and date you called. If this initial action fails to get the response you were looking for, write to the lender clearly outlining the complaint and how you want it resolved. You should address the letter to the particular branch involved. This will then be investigated by their internal complaints procedure. If the lender has not made an error, they will supply you with the relevant information to prove this. If they have made an error, they should pay you reasonable compensation for your time spent in addressing this problem. If the lender is uncooperative, taking a long time to resolve the matter, or you are unhappy with their response, you should then contact the relevant ombudsman.

Using an ombudsman or arbitrator

The majority of lenders will be members of either the Council of Mortgage Lenders or the Banking or Building Societies Ombudsmen schemes. There are various ombudsman who deal with the different lenders:

- building societies – the Building Societies Ombudsman
- banks – the Banking Ombudsman
- any other institution or intermediary – Chartered Institute of Arbitrators.

The address and telephone numbers for these ombudsmen are located at the back of this book under Useful Addresses. The service an ombudsman provides is free. Do not contact an ombudsman unless the complaint you have lodged with the lender's internal complaints procedure has been exhausted.

The ombudsman will contact the lender and request an answer to your complaint within a specific time period. Should the ombudsman find the lender at fault, the ombudsman will then instruct the lender to pay compensation to you. If the ombudsman decides against your claim, you will receive written notice outlining the reasons for this.

Taking the case further

If the lender is not a member of an ombudsman or arbitration scheme, or you are not satisfied with the outcome from an ombudsman or arbitrator, you can take the matter further. You should seek advice from your local Citizens' Advice Bureau (CAB) or Trading Standards Department. Like the ombudsman and arbitration schemes, this advice is free. These particular organisations can offer you good advice and advise you whether your case is worth pursuing. Should you decide to take the case further and involve a solicitor, you will be charged fees for their services.

LOCATING HELP FOR FINANCIAL DIFFICULTIES

Many people throughout their lives may find themselves in a tight spot from time to time due to losing a job, ill heath and so on. There are three golden rules you should obey at the first sign of any financial difficulty:

1. Contact your lender immediately and discuss the problem with them.
2. Do not ignore the problem, as it will escalate beyond proportions.
3. Never borrow, especially at high interest rates, in order to make payments to your mortgage, as this will only make your financial position worse.

Contacting the lender

Many people fail to contact a lender, resulting in the lender contacting them. Why don't they call? Because of pride usually, so put pride aside and call them. Lenders can be sympathetic to genuine cases. If a lender has to contact you, this may affect your credit rating. Most companies will negotiate reduced payments in genuine cases. If your financial position involves a number of debts, it may pay to seek advice first.

Obtaining advice

If you find yourself in a serious financial position with multiple debts, there are many organisations that can offer you advice. Your local Citizens' Advice Bureau (CAB), the Federation of Independent Advice Centres and National Debtline are all organisations that may be able to help. The addresses and phone numbers are located at the back of this book under Useful Addresses.

Seeking financial support
There are many government and state benefits you may be entitled to. Contact your local social security office to discuss your situation with them. Once again, put pride aside – the sooner you deal with your problems the sooner you can resolve them.

CASE STUDIES

Natalie receives an unexpected bill
Since Natalie's new mortgage was settled, she has received a bill from the mortgage broker for their fees for assisting her. When Natalie initially spoke with the mortgage broker, they did not disclose these fees as they should have done under the Mortgage Code. Natalie called the broker to lodge her complaint. The broker contacted her promptly and told her to disregard the letter they sent as it was an administration error. Natalie knew they could not enforce the fee anyway as the broker did not disclose the fee to her. She is glad she chose one that subscribes to the Mortgage Code.

John lodges a complaint
Having recently established a mortgage with a new bank, John has just received a mortgage statement for the first month. Looking closely at the statement he finds a charge he does not recognise. Looking at the tariff the lender gave him, he finds that this fee is unwarranted. He contacts the branch he is dealing with and lodges a complaint, and also sends a letter outlining the complaint. A week goes by and he does not receive a response from the lender. He decides to contact the lender and is told that they are extremely busy at the moment but they will try to get to his complaint as soon as possible. Two more weeks go by and still nothing. Once again he contacts the lender and they have no answer for him. He then decides to contact the banking ombudsman, completes the necessary forms and sends them to the ombudsman. The ombudsman contacts him a few days later and tells him that the lender has accepted it is their fault. Shortly after he receives a phone call from the manager of the bank's branch and he apologises for the discrepancy. The manager explains that they had a systems error

which affected many people's statements and the sheer volume of complaints slowed their response times. The manager once again apologised and told John the charge would be removed by the end of the working day.

Ross contacts the lender

Because of the lack of homework, Ross did not allow for all the associated costs of buying a house. This resulted in him having to scrape together every available resource he had, placing unnecessary financial strain on him. Since paying the mortgage payments he has not been able to get ahead and with the prospects of a baby on the way he is worried. Ross has decided to contact the lender and see what they can do. Having talked his case over with the lender's manager, the lender has decided to reduce the monthly repayments for three months to help him get back on his feet. Ross now realises, with hindsight, that he should have done more homework rather than rushing in and buying a property. Getting caught up in the excitement of their first house caused them a lot of problems which could have been avoided.

QUESTIONS AND ANSWERS

Can I hand the keys back to the lender and walk away from the property?

This would have to be the worst thing a person could do. Even though you have walked away, you will still remain totally liable to the mortgage until it is settled. If you take this course of action, you will have to pay all the interest that accrues on the mortgage until the property is sold. You will be liable for the costs of selling the property and any shortfall between what the property is sold for and the outstanding debt. You may then be taken to court to repay the shortfall amount and the legal costs. Finally, you may destroy any chances of obtaining credit in the future.

If I negotiate lower payments with my lender, will I still have to pay interest?

Yes, if you do find yourself in financial difficulties and you negotiate reduced payments, the lender may add the interest charges to the mortgage balance. As a result your mortgage balance will increase.

PERSONAL MORTGAGE AUDIT

- What action would you take if you could not afford to repay your mortgage repayment?

- Do you have any mortgage protection insurances in place to protect yourself against any unforeseen events, e.g. losing your job, sickness or disability? Do you think this protection would reduce the chances of financial hardship?

- If you are presently in a position of financial hardship, are you claiming all the benefits you are entitled to? What positive plans do you have to resolve the situation?

Glossary

Amortisation. The period of time a loan is scheduled to be repaid in full. Also known as the **scheduled repayment term**.

Amortisation schedule. Provides a breakdown of the interest payments, any capital or principal reduction and the balance outstanding at any given point during the scheduled repayment term of a loan.

APR or **annual percentage rate**. Used to provide consumers with the true annual cost of a loan, expressed as a percentage. It incorporates all establishment and ongoing costs of the mortgage. Because lenders calculate them differently, they should not be relied upon alone to gauge the total cost of the loan.

ATM or **automated teller machines**. Electronic cash machines.

Capital. The amount of money borrowed from a lender.

Capital and interest repayment. With each repayment made, a portion of the capital and the interest charge is repaid, until the capital is repaid in full.

Capped rate. An interest rate charged over a specified period of time which can rise and fall, but cannot rise above a capped interest rate.

Cash back. An amount of money paid by a lender when a mortgage is taken out. The amount can be a lump sum or a percentage of the amount borrowed.

Charge. 1. The legal right a lender has over a property used as security, until the borrowed amount has been repaid in full. 2. Any fee a lender imposes for the use of borrowed funds or services rendered.

Collar. Used in conjunction with **capped** interest rates. It prevents the interest rate falling below a set interest rate. (The interest rate may be capped at 8 per cent and may also be collared at 6 per cent.) This prevents the borrower from enjoying lower rates should they fall below the collared rate.

Glossary

Commission. A payment made to advisers, brokers and intermediaries for selling or providing goods and services.

Credit reference. Information gathered by credit reference agencies about an individual's financial standing, for use by organisations to assess their risk profile.

Current account. An account which generally has a cheque book and other facilities that an ordinary savings account may not have. This type of account generally pays a lower rate of interest than a savings account.

Debit card. A card which can be used to purchase goods and services, the cost of which is debited directly from available funds in your account. No credit facility is available on a debit card.

Deposit account. This type of account generally pays a higher rate of interest than a *current account*, but may restrict access to funds. They do not normally have cheque book and other facilities that a current account provides.

Discharge. When a mortgage has been paid in full and the charge is removed from a property.

Discounted rate. A guaranteed reduction in the standard variable interest rate over a specified period. Once the specified period ends the discounted rate usually reverts to the prevailing variable interest rate at that time.

Endowment. A life assurance policy providing a lump sum amount, designed to pay off an interest-only mortgage. There are different types of endowment policies available, such as 'with profits', 'unit linked' and 'unit linked with profits'.

Equity. For a homeowner, this term is used in relation to the difference between what the property is valued at and the amount of any loans secured against it.

Fixed rate. This is where the interest rate is set for an agreed amount over a specified term of months or years. During the specified term, regardless of whether interest rates rise or fall, a fixed interest rate will remain static.

Gross of tax. Where no tax has been deducted, 'before tax'.

IFA or **independent financial adviser.** One who is not tied to just one organisation supplying investments, insurances or mortgage products. They give independent and impartial advice, providing various products from a variety of sources that are most suitable for the individual's needs.

Interest. The cost of using borrowed money, expressed as a percentage. Interest is charged on the amount you borrow, i.e. the **capital/principal**.

Interest-only repayment. The repayment to the lender is just interest. None of the monthly repayment is used to repay the capital/principal of the loan. Generally an investment or savings plan is used to repay the capital in the future.

ISA or **individual savings plan.** Set to replace the **personal equity plan** or **PEP** in 1999. These savings plans are highly flexible, tax effective investments, allowing up to £7,000 to be invested in the first year, and £5,000 per year thereafter.

LTV or **loan-to-value ratio.** The amount borrowed expressed as a percentage of the property purchase price, or property valuation (whichever is the lower). (A £75,000 mortgage secured on a property valued at £100,000 would result in an LTV of 75 per cent.)

MIG or **mortgage indemnity guarantee premium.** This insurance protects the lender against any losses should they exercise their power of sale and repossess your home. Lenders will generally charge a MIG premium if the LTV ratio is high.

MIRAS or **mortgage interest relief at source.** Tax relief given to mortgage interest payments on the first £30,000. The relief given at present is 10 per cent.

Mortgage. A loan used to buy a home, whereby the property is used as security, until the original amount borrowed is paid in full.

Mortgagee. The entity borrowing the money, the borrower. Can be a natural person, company and so on.

Mortgagor. The institution lending the money, the lender.

Negative equity. When the total amount of loans secured on a property exceeds the property's value. Basically you owe more money than the property is worth.

Net of tax. Where tax has already been deducted, 'after tax'.

Ombudsman. An independent official who investigates complaints against service providers.

PEP or **personal equity plan.** An investment where the income and gains are free from taxation and capital gains tax. Can be used to repay an interest-only mortgage.

Personal pension. A savings plan and investment used to provide an income in retirement years. A portion of a personal pension (the tax free lump sum) can be used to pay off an interest-only mortgage.

Premiums. Contributions made to an insurance policy or investment.

Principal. The amount of money borrowed from a lender (capital).

Redemption penalties. Charges imposed by a lender for the partial or full discharge of a mortgage.

Repossession. Where a lender exercises its power of sale and repossesses a property if the borrower has drastically fallen behind in mortgage repayments.

Savings account. An account that pays higher interest than a **current account**, but may not have a cheque book. There may be restrictions for accessing funds.

Stamp duty. A government tax payable on the transfer of ownership of a property with a purchase price above £60,000.

Subsidy. Money granted, to subsidise.

Tariff. A list of fees a lender will charge for the services they provide.

Term. The life span of a contract to repay an amount of money in full.

Tied agent. Individuals or organisations who sell products and services from a particular company. They do not provide independent and impartial advice.

Valuation. A check of the property in order to determine its value. Lenders will carry out valuations on properties to assess whether they are suitable for a mortgage.

Variable rate. The interest rate the lender charges which fluctuates with the market. A variable rate can rise and fall depending on market conditions.

The Personal Investment Authority Ombudsman, 3rd Floor, Centre Point, 103 New Oxford Street, London WC1A 1QH. Tel: (0171) 538 8860.

Further Reading

Dealing With Your Bank, Brian Cain (How To Books, 1997).
Managing Your Personal Finances, John Claxton (How To Books, 1998, 2nd edition).
Your Home, Diana Wright (Harper Collins, 1996).
Negative Equity – What Can I Do? National Debtline (1995).
Which? Way to Buy, Sell and Move House, Consumers Association (1993).
Saving and Investing, John Whiteley (How To Books, 1998).
Arranging Insurance, Terry Hallett (How To Books, 1997).

There are a few monthly publications available in bookshops and newsagents, containing up-to-date information on various lenders, interest rate deals and much more:

What Mortgage, Charterhouse Communications Ltd.
Your Mortgage, Matching Hat Ltd.
Moneyfacts, Moneyfacts Publications.

Index

advisers, 94–96
amortisation, 22
annualised repayments scheme, 30
application process, 112–116
APR, 23–24

banks, 91
building societies, 90–91

capital, 21
capital repayment mortgage, 22, 52–54, 72, 79, 82–83
capped interest rates, 31–32
cash back, 59–60
centralised lenders, 92–93
cocktail loans, 70–71
collared interest rates, 31
complaints, 121–123
consolidating debts, 69–70
credit cards, 83–84
credit references, 115–116
current account mortgage, 80–83

deposit, 63–64, 99
discounted interest rates, 32

endowment insurance, 45–46, 55–57
expenses checklist, 110–112

fixed interest rate, 30–31
flexible mortgage, 75–80
fortnightly payments, 65–66

honeymoon rates, 32

incentives, 59–60
income, 108–110
income multiplier, 109
interest rates, 23, 25–28, 44–45
interest calculation, 25–30
interest charging, 25, 28–30
interest only mortgage, 22–23, 54–55, 79–80, 83
ISA, 58

land registry fee, 101
local authority searches, 101

MIRAS, 35–37
mortgage brokers, 95
Mortgage Code, The, 87–89, 95
mortgage indemnity guarantee, 37–39, 64
mortgage protection insurance, 39–40
mortgage statement, 120
mortgagee, 21
mortgagor, 21

negative equity, 17, 106–107
new way of banking, 81

134

Index

overpayments, 67, 77–78

payment holiday, 78
pension, 45–46, 58–59
PEP, 45–46, 57
principal, 21

redemption penalties, 32–34, 102
refinancing, 72, 102–106

savings history, 99
savings plans, 71–72
scheduled repayment term, 22, 64–65
self employed, 110

specialist lenders, 92–93
splitting a mortgage, 70–71
stamp duty, 100
surplus funds, 77–78
surveyors, 101

tariff, 120–121
ties & compulsories, 60
traditional banking system 46–48

valuation, 101
variable interest rates, 30

weekly payments, 66–67